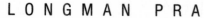

LONGMAN PRA

GW01080097

PERSONAL INJURY

1ST EDITION

Nicholas Saunders, MA (OXON)
Solicitor, Head of Legal Education,
The Law Society

SERIES EDITOR
CM Brand, Solicitor and Lecturer in Law,
University of Liverpool

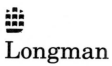

Longman

© Longman Group UK Ltd 1988

Published by

Longman Group UK Ltd
21/27 Lamb's Conduit Street
London WC1N 3NJ

Associated Offices:

Australia, Hong Kong, Malaysia, Singapore, USA

ISBN 0 85121 4487

A CIP catalogue record for this book is available
from the British Library

Printed in Great Britain by Biddles Ltd, Guildford, Surrey.

PREFACE

This introduction to the practice and procedure of personal injury claims was written at a time of great actual and forthcoming change. While it was not practicable to anticipate changes likely to result from the Lord Chancellor's Civil Justice Review, I have assumed that the transfer of responsibility for the Legal Aid Scheme under the Legal Aid Bill 1988 will go ahead. I have taken account of amendments to the Bill in the Second Reading in the Lords. However, until early 1989 readers should take references to the Legal Aid Board as references to the Law Society Legal Aid Administration.

I should like to thank my colleagues Ian Storey for his comments on the likely changes to be made by the Legal Aid Bill, and John Hodgson for reading the book in proof. Finally, I should like to thank my family for their patience while the book was written.

The law is stated as at 4 June 1988.

Nicholas Saunders
June 1988

CONTENTS

9 Early conclusion of cases

CHAPTER 1

BASIC INFORMATION

The law on which personal injury actions are based is fundamentally the common law of negligence, but this is overlaid by many different statutes according to the factual context of the claim.

1.1 General principles

1.1.1 Negligence Most personal injury actions are pleaded in negligence. Accordingly, the plaintiff must show, on the balance of probabilities, the existence of a duty of care owed by the defendant to him and breach of that duty causing him damage which was not too legally remote. Quite often cases are lost through failure to ensure that all these points are satisfied.

On the duty of care, note that a child born alive but disabled as a result of an event which affected either parent's ability to have a normal child will be able to sue if the parent would have been able to (Congenital Disabilities (Civil Liability) Act 1976, s 1).

The plaintiff may recover damages for nervous shock, ie medically recognised psychiatric disorder, as well as, or in the absence of, physical injuries, if injury by shock is foreseeable (*McLoughlin* v *O'Brian* [1982] 2 All ER 298; *Attia* v *British Gas* [1987] 3 WLR 1101).

The Crown is generally liable in tort under the Crown Proceedings Act 1947. This now includes injuries to members of the armed forces resulting from their colleagues' negligence during active service (Crown Proceedings Act 1987). Whether the Crown (including bodies such as health authorities) is liable for breach of statutory duty depends on the particular statute concerned.

The duty is only to take reasonable care. The flexibility of the standard is shown by situations such as sporting events, where it may be easier for the defendant to show he or she took reasonable care to avoid harm to players (*Condon* v *Basi* [1985] 2 All ER 457) and in the case of children the standard is adjusted for the child's age (*Gorely* v *Codd* [1967] 1 WLR 19).

Proof of breach of the standard may be helped by the maxim *res ipsa loquitur* if the accident was caused by something under the defendant's control (such as a car) and was something that would not

1

normally happen without negligence (such as the car running into a tree) the court may give the plaintiff judgment in the absence of contrary evidence. However, the onus of proof remains on the plaintiff (*Ng Chun Pui* v *Lee Chuen Tat* (1988) *The Times* 25 May)

The basic test of causation is whether the plaintiff's harm would not have occurred but for the defendant's negligence. However, several causes may satisfy this test. Where they each contribute to the harm but are not each sufficient in themselves, the plaintiff can sue all the tortfeasors (normally better tactically). Alternatively, the plaintiff can sue any one of them, leaving that defendant to recover from the other persons at fault a contribution or indemnity for the damages he has paid to the plaintiff (Civil Liability (Contribution) Act 1978). However, the position is more difficult where each factor might have been sufficient in itself to have caused the injury (see 1.6.2).

1.1.2 Breach of statutory duty For the plaintiff to be able to recover compensation it must be shown that the statute intended to create a right to compensation, that the plaintiff is within the type of persons that the statute intended to benefit and that the damage was of the type that the statute was intended to guard against. These questions can only be decided in the context of the particular statute.

Causation must also be established as in negligence cases.

1.1.3 Vicarious liability To hold the employer liable the person committing the tort must have been employed under a contract of service, not a contract for services, and acting in the course of the employment, ie on the master's business and not a 'frolic of his own'.

Where there is vicarious liability, the employer and employee are jointly and severally liable to the plaintiff. As the employer under the Employers' Liability (Compulsory Insurance) Act 1969 must be insured against third party claims, it is common to sue only the employer, having first obtained an undertaking from the employer's insurers or their solicitors that vicarious liability will not be disputed. The employer will then be entitled to claim an indemnity from the negligent employee, but employers' liability insurers have made a 'gentlemen's agreement' not to pursue these rights in the absence of collusion or wilful misconduct (which is rare).

Similar principles may apply where a chattel, (eg a car), is loaned by the owner to the defendant for the owner's purposes (*Morgans* v *Launchbury* [1973] AC 127).

1.1.4 Liability for acts of independent contractors It is normally enough if the defendant has employed apparently competent contractors (*Cassidy* v *Minister of Health* [1951] 2 KB 343) unless the defendant was under a non-delegable duty to ensure care was taken (see 1.5).

1.2 Road accidents

1.2.1 Substantive law The usual arguments are over whether the driver's duty of care to other road users has been broken, whether any breach has caused the plaintiff's loss and as to any contributory negligence by the plaintiff.

Where the defendant has been convicted of a relevant driving offence, the burden of proof is effectively reversed by Civil Evidence Act 1968, s 11. This requires the defendant to show that the conviction was wrong or irrelevant, eg because the offence of driving with defective brakes was one of strict liability and the defendant had no warning of the brake failure.

The standard expected is that of the reasonably careful and competent qualified driver (*Nettleship* v *Weston* [1971] 2 QB 691). The driver must anticipate the negligence of others where experience suggests this is common, but can assume that generally other motorists will obey fundamental rules of the road such as stopping at red traffic lights (*Tremayne* v *Hill* [1987] RTR 131, CA). Pedestrians also have a duty to take reasonable care (*Fitzgerald* v *Lane* (1988) *The Independent* 14 July, HL. The Highway Code is admissible to show the practice of reasonably careful road users (Road Traffic Act 1972, s 37).

Where several vehicles are involved it may be very difficult to establish exactly which vehicles did what damage. The court may look at the matter broadly as being one event to avoid these problems (*Fitzgerald* v *Lane*, above).

For the liability of highway authorities for injuries due to their failure to keep the highway in repair, see the Highways Act 1980, ss 41, 58.

1.2.2 Insurance and compensation schemes Drivers using a motor vehicle on a public road should have insurance against claims by third parties for personal injuries and death (Road Traffic Act 1972, s 143). Judgments for such losses can be enforced against the insurers, even if the insurers were entitled to or have in fact avoided the policy, eg for misrepresentation by their insured. Notice must have been given before or within seven days of taking proceedings (Road Traffic Act, s 149). Enforcement against insurers is also possible if the third party has gone bankrupt or into liquidation (Third Parties (Rights against Insurers) Act 1930).

However, this will not apply if the driver was uninsured, eg because the policy was allowed to lapse or if at the time of the accident the use of the vehicle was not covered by the policy. In this situation the judgment will have to be enforced against the Motor Insurers' Bureau under the Uninsured Drivers Agreement. Seven days' notice of the proceedings must be given to the MIB.

If the driver cannot be traced but it is possible to show that the accident was the fault of the untraced driver, a claim can be made to the MIB under the Untraced Driver Agreement. The MIB will instruct a member insurer to investigate the claim, liability and quantum having to be proved in the usual way. There is an appeal by way of arbitration to a QC.

If the accident was the result of a deliberate attempt to injure, the uninsured driver agreement will apply but not the untraced driver agreement. An application to the Criminal Injuries Compensation Board can, however, be made.

Under the insurance policy, the insurers will normally have rights to be informed of any claims against the insured person and to nominate solicitors to deal with those claims. If they pay a claim under the policy, eg for repairs to their insured's vehicle, they have the right of subrogation, ie to take proceedings in their insured's name against any other person who may be liable, to recover the amount paid.

Uninsured losses, such as any no claims bonus or 'excess' (the first £50 or other agreed part of the claim) will not be recoverable from the insurers and will have to be claimed from the defendant as an item of special damage. Insurers may also try to avoid disputes with third parties and their insurers by making 'knock for knock' agreements under which each insurer pays its own insured for his or her losses. However, clients should be warned that these agreements are not legally binding on them and that they may cause them to lose their no claims bonus.

1.3 Dangerous premises

The liability of occupiers to lawful visitors is regulated by the Occupiers Liability Act 1957. The 'common duty of care' owed to all visitors (s 2(1)) is very similar to the common law of negligence. The degree of care will vary with the type of visitor, so occupiers must expect children to be less careful than adults (s 2(3) (a)). The occupier is entitled to expect that a person in the exercise of his or her calling will guard against any special risks ordinarily incidental to it, but see *Ogwo* v *Taylor* [1987] 3 WLR 1145, HL.

Finally, where the damage results from the negligence of an independent contractor, the occupier will generally not be liable if reasonable care was taken in selecting and supervising the contractor
(*Ferguson* v *Welsh* [1987] 3 All ER 777, HL).

The liability of occupiers to persons other than lawful visitors, eg
trespassers, is governed by the Occupiers Liability Act 1984. The
occupier will owe a duty to take reasonable care to see the non-visitor
does not suffer injury if the occupier ought to know of the danger and
that the non-visitor is likely to be in the vicinity and it is reasonable
to expect the non-visitor to be offered some protection.

Landlords will also often owe a duty of reasonable care towards
entrants under the Defective Premises Act 1972, s 4.

The liability of other persons with regard to dangerous premises,
eg independent contractors, builders and architects, is governed by
the common law of negligence.

There are numerous statutory provisions dealing with the safety
of buildings. Many of these, such as the Guard Dogs Act and the Fire
Precautions Act 1971 and Fire Safety and Safety of Places of Sport
Act 1987 are enforceable by criminal law only. However, the Building
Act 1980 and building regulations made thereunder are enforceable
by actions for damages in tort.

1.4   Dangerous products

A purchaser of a defective product that causes that person injury will
normally have a remedy under the sale contract, particularly because
of the terms of merchantable quality and reasonable fitness for
purpose implied into sales in the course of a business by the Sale of
Goods Act 1979. Formerly, where the plaintiff was not the purchaser,
he or she would have had to rely largely on the possibility of showing
that the manufacturer was negligent.

However, the Consumer Protection Act 1987 (which replaces the
much more limited Consumer Safety Act 1978) creates strict liability
for defective products (though note the 'state of the art' defence
discussed in 1.8.5). Although the plaintiff may not have had any
contract with the defendant, and may be unable to prove that the
defendant was at fault, the producers (ie the manufacturers of the
whole or the relevant component of the product), any 'own-branders'
who put their name on the product, or the first importers into the
EEC can be held liable. If none of these are identifiable, the plaintiff
can sue the supplier (s 2).

Products do not include agricultural products that have not under-
gone an industrial process. A product is defective if its safety is not

5

such as persons generally are entitled to expect, having regard to any warnings given with the product (s 3(1)). Damage includes death, personal injury and loss of or damage to property excluding the defective product itself exceeding £275 (s 5(1)). The Congenital Disabilities (Civil Liability) Act 1976 applies (s 6).

1.5 Factory accidents

Employers may be liable vicariously for the negligence of other employees acting in the course of their employment, personally for breach of non-delegable common law duties, or for breach of statutory duty. Vicarious liability has already been dealt with in 1.1.3. Finally, apart from holding the employer liable, it may be possible to seek a payment from the state under the Pneumoconiosis Etc (Workers' Compensation) Act 1979 in the case of certain prescribed diseases.

1.5.1 Common law duties The employer owes personal, non-delegable duties to employees (*McDermid* v *Nash Dredging and Reclamation* [1987] AC 906, HL) to provide safe plant and machinery (Employers' Liability (Defective Equipment) Act 1969, s 1(1)); to provide a safe place of work; to provide a safe system of work; and to provide a reasonably competent and properly instructed staff. These duties, however, are only to do what is reasonable and employees too are expected to take reasonable care for their own safety (*Smith* v *Scott Bowyers* [1986] IRLR 315, CA).

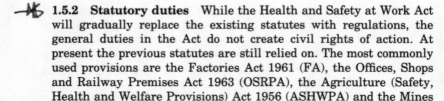 **1.5.2 Statutory duties** While the Health and Safety at Work Act will gradually replace the existing statutes with regulations, the general duties in the Act do not create civil rights of action. At present the previous statutes are still relied on. The most commonly used provisions are the Factories Act 1961 (FA), the Offices, Shops and Railway Premises Act 1963 (OSRPA), the Agriculture (Safety, Health and Welfare Provisions) Act 1956 (ASHWPA) and the Mines and Quarries Act 1954 (MQA).

The duties most often relevant are:

- To fence machinery, dangerous substances and openings in floors (FA, ss 12–14, 18, 28(4); OSRPA, s 17; regulations under ASHWPA; MQA, s 81).
- To ensure floors, passages and stairs are sound, free from obstruction and not slippery (FA, s 28(1); MQA, s 34; OSRPA, s 16).
- To remove dust and fumes (FA, s 63; MQA, s 55(1)).
- Not to require lifting of heavy weights (FA, s 72; OSRPA, s 23).

The standard of care varies. For example, the duty to fence under

FA, s 14(1) is absolute, whereas the duty to keep floors clear and non-slippery under FA, s 28(1) is only so far as is reasonably practicable.

Where the employer is convicted of breach of the statutes or regulations this can be pleaded in a civil action under Civil Evidence Act 1968, s 11.

1.6   Medical negligence

The difficulties here relate to the standard of care, causation and evidence. The last is dealt with in Chapter 4. Note also the possibility of obtaining payments from the state under the Vaccine Damage Payments Act 1979.

1.6.1   Standard of care   The doctor's duty is not to cure the patient but to conform to the standard of a reasonably competent person exercising and professing to have that skill. It appears that the standard will be that appropriate to the function that the defendant performs: a houseman will be judged by the standard applicable to a junior doctor and not to a consultant (*Wilsher* v *Essex Area Health Authority* [1987] 3 QB 730, CA). The doctor must keep up to date, but will not be liable if he or she has acted in accordance with a practice accepted as proper by a responsible body of doctors skilled in that area, even if some doctors would have acted differently (*Bolam* v *Friern Hospital Management Committee* [1952] 2 All ER 118). This applies to all aspects of medicine, including diagnosis, treatment and advice (*Gold* v *Haringey Health Authority* [1987] 3 All ER 649, CA).

1.6.2   Causation   Negligence will not be actionable if the plaintiff would have suffered the harm in any event (*Kay* v *Ayrshire and Arran Health Board* [1987] 2 All ER 417, HL). If the chance of recovery would otherwise have been less than 50 per cent the defendant's negligence will not be regarded as causing the loss, and no damages can be awarded: the plaintiff cannot recover a proportion of the damages for the loss of a chance of recovery less than 50 per cent (*Hotson* v *East Berkshire Health Authority* [1987] 2 All ER 910, HL). If there are several possible causes the court cannot in the absence of evidence infer that the negligent one was the cause of the loss (*Wilsher* v *Essex Area Health Authority* [1988] All ER 871, HL).

1.7   Fatal accidents

1.7.1   Law Reform (Miscellaneous Provisions) Act 1934   This provides that where either party dies, existing causes of action survive against or for the benefit of the estate of the deceased (s 1(4)). An action brought by the estate of a deceased plaintiff is dealt with on the same basis as if the plaintiff were alive. The measure of damages is generally the same (but see 2.5).

1.7.2 Fatal Accidents Act 1976 This gives the deceased's dependants a cause of action for the loss of their dependency if the deceased would have had an action had he or she survived, having regard, eg, to any defence that the defendant would have had.

The dependants who can sue are:

- Spouses, former spouses and cohabitees for the last two years.
- Parents or grand-parents.
- Children or grand-children, including any child treated by the deceased as his own and step-children; illegitimate children are treated as the children of the mother and reputed father.
- Brothers, sisters, uncles, aunts or their issue.

These relationships include relationships by marriage and half-blood (s 1).

The action is usually brought by the personal representatives of the deceased, if there is no conflict of interest, in conjunction with the 1934 Act claim, but if no action is started within six months of the deceased's death any dependant can sue on behalf of all the dependants (s 2).

For the measure of damages, see 2.6.

1.8 Defences

Generally, the onus of proof of these defences is on the defendant.

1.8.1 Contributory negligence The courts can apportion liability where harm has been caused partly by the fault of the defendant and partly by that of the plaintiff (Law Reform (Contributory Negligence) Act 1945, s 1(1)).

The defendant must raise the point in the defence. It must be shown that the plaintiff failed to take reasonable care and that this contributed either to the accident or to the damage, eg by failing to wear a seat belt (*Froom* v *Butcher* [1976] QB 286) (25 per cent, deduction if the belt would have prevented the injuries, 15 per cent if it would have reduced them) or by accepting a lift knowing the defendant had been drinking (*Owens* v *Brimmell* [1977] QB 859). It seems that these figures have been unaffected by the requirement in the Motor Vehicles (Wearing of Seat Belts) Regulations 1982 that those in the front seats of motor vehicles must wear seat belts.

The defence is applied in the light of the plaintiff's age and physical but not mental condition. It is less likely to apply in actions for breach of statutory duty which are designed to protect workers from their own carelessness, although 100 per cent contributory negligence is possible even here (*Jayes* v *IMI Kynoch Ltd* [1985] IRLR 155).

The court reduces the plaintiff's damages to the extent it thinks just and reasonable having regard to the plaintiff's share in the responsibility for the damage, assessed in terms of causation (*Fitzgerald* v *Lane* [1987] 2 All ER 455, CA) or, more commonly, the parties' relative degree of culpability (*Westwood* v *Post Office* [1974] AC 1).

1.8.2 Volenti non fit injuria This means a voluntary agreement by the plaintiff, made with knowledge of the nature and extent of the risk, to absolve the defendant from legal liability for the results of an unreasonable risk of harm.

Because of economic pressures, volenti will rarely be available in employers' liability actions (*ICI* v *Shatwell* [1965] AC 656). Nor will it probably apply to accepting lifts from drunken or incompetent drivers (*Dann* v *Hamilton* [1939] 1 KB 509). Notices in cars that travel is at the passenger's own risk are ineffective (Road Traffic Act 1972, s 148(3)). However, the defence may be available to occupiers, at least with regard to non-visitors (*Titchener* v *British Railways Board* [1983] 3 All ER 770).

The plaintiff must have had actual knowledge of both the nature and extent of the risk. However, doctors do not have a duty to warn a patient of all the risks of treatment, but only those that a reasonably careful doctor would mention (*Sidaway* v *Bethlem Royal Hospital Governors* [1985] 1 All ER 643, HL).

The consent needed for the defence to succeed in negligence actions is not to the risk of injury as such but to the lack of reasonable care that may produce that risk (*Wooldridge* v *Sumner* [1963] 2 QB 43). Thus the defence will not often succeed in ordinary negligence cases.

1.8.3 Exclusion clauses These are now ineffective in relation to liability for death or personal injury to motor vehicle passengers (see 1.7.2.). Further, attempts to exclude such liability arising in the course of a business from negligence are ineffective (Unfair Contract Terms Act 1977, s 2(1)) though duties stricter than negligence can be excluded. In respect of other losses exclusion is valid only if reasonable (s 2(2)).

1.8.4 Limitation

- General. This is a *vital point* in personal injury cases. Failure by the plaintiff to issue proceedings within the limitation period and to serve them within a further twelve months is the single biggest cause of professional negligence claims in civil litigation. It is *essential* to make a prominent diary and file note of the expiry of these periods and to have a procedure for regularly reviewing all files to check that such dates have not been missed. A master index of such dates, on computer if necessary, is a good back-up.

  Limitation must be pleaded by the defendant if it is to be relied on. It is not for the plaintiff to apply to have the matter dealt with before the action can proceed (*Kennet* v *Brown* (1988) *The Times*, 10 March, CA). However, limitation is normally taken as a preliminary point before the substantive issues are tried. The statutes are consolidated in the Limitation Act 1980.

- The basic period. In personal injury actions this is three years from either the date of accrual of the cause of action (ie when the damage occurs) *or*, if later, the date of the plaintiff's knowledge that the injury was significant and attributable to the defendant's breach of duty (s 14(1)). An injury is significant if it would have been reasonable to take proceedings in respect of it (s 14(2)). Knowledge includes that which the plaintiff could reasonably be expected to acquire himself or with the help of expert advice (s 14(3)).

- Overriding the time bar. The court has the discretion to allow the action to proceed after the expiry of the basic period if it is equitable to do so having regard to the degree to which the time bar prejudices the plaintiff and the degree to which overriding it will prejudice the defendant (s 33(1)). The court must look at all the circumstances including the length of and reasons for delay, the effect on the cogency of the evidence and any steps the plaintiff has taken to obtain expert advice. The discretion is unfettered (*Thompson* v *Brown Construction (Ebbw Vale) Ltd* [1981] 2 All ER 296, HL). However, if the plaintiff tries to start a second action after starting one within time which has been struck out for want of prosecution, s 33 will not apply *Walkley* v *Precision Forgings* [1979] 1 WLR 606, HL).

- Fatal accidents. Under both the 1934 and 1976 Acts, if the deceased died before the expiry of the limitation period, then a three-year period runs from the date of death or the date of knowledge of the personal representatives or dependants. When this expires an application can be made under s 33. If the deceased's limitation period had expired, then the personal representatives or dependants must apply under s 33.

- Consumer Protection Act. The usual rules apply with an absolute ten-year 'long stop' (Consumer Protection Act 1987, Sch 1).
- Compensation schemes. The time limit is three years from the event giving rise to the injury under both the MIB, and CICB schemes. The MIB (but not the CICB) will entertain a late application in exceptional circumstances.
- Minors and mental patients.   Time does not run until the plaintiff reaches eighteen, ceases to be of unsound mind or dies, whichever happens first (Limitation Act 1980, s 28(1)).

1.8.5   Illegality   In some circumstances the defendant may be able to rely on the maxim that a person cannot profit from his or her own wrong (*Cummings* v *Grainger* [1977] 1 All ER 104).

The CICB may reduce or refuse any award on the ground of the plaintiff's character, conduct or way of life.

1.8.6   'State of the art'   Under s 4(1) (*e*) of the Consumer Protection Act 1987 it is a defence if the state of scientific and technical knowledge was not such that a producer of products of the same description as the product in question might be expected to have discovered the defect.

Similarly, the state of knowledge in the industry or profession at the time will be relevant to whether the defendant employer provided a safe system of work, or took such steps as were reasonably practicable under Factories Act 1961, s 29(1) or as were practicable under Mines and Quarries Act 1954, s 157 or whether a doctor was negligent in not using a new technique.

1.9   Jurisdiction

Whereas the jurisdiction of the High Court is unlimited, both in the amount of the claim and geographically, that of the county court is limited in both respects. In contract and tort actions, the maximum claim that can be brought in the county court is £5000. Actions must be brought in the county court where the cause of action arose, ie for the area where the accident happened, or for that where the *defendant* lives or carries on business.

Cases for any amount can be brought in the High Court but the bringing of smaller cases that could have been brought in the county court is discouraged by County Courts Act 1984, ss 19 and 20. These provide that if the plaintiff in the High Court recovers less than £3000 he or she will be entitled only to costs on the county court scale and if the plaintiff recovers less than £600 he or she will not be entitled to any costs, unless the High Court feels that there were reasonable grounds for thinking that more than £5000 would be recovered. For the purposes of ss 19 and 20 contributory negligence and interest are ignored.

On the question of which court to choose for claims which may be worth between £3000 and £5000 see 4.7.2. However, note here that the High Court is increasingly using its powers to transfer cases to the county court even where they are likely to exceed £5000 where it thinks they are suitable for trial there. By the same token, the court should be prepared to allow county court cases to be transferred up to the High Court where it becomes clear that they are more difficult or substantial than at first thought.

CHAPTER 2

DAMAGES AND INTEREST

This chapter will deal with the types of loss for which damages can be claimed in personal injury actions and how the extent of such losses is assessed.

For a more detailed coverage of these topics see Kemp, *Damages for Personal Injury and Death.*

A major distinction must be made between general damages, ie those which cannot be precisely quantified in the pleadings and can only be assessed by the judge, and special damages, which can (and must) be quantified and pleaded by the party claiming them.

2.1 Heads of general damages

These should not be specifically pleaded; it is not appropriate to claim, say, £3000 for the plaintiff's broken leg. However, enough information must be given to enable the judge to assess the damages. Thus the statement or particulars of claim should contain particulars of the plaintiff's injuries and treatment, any special effect of the injuries on the plaintiff and the plaintiff's date of birth.

The main heads of general damages are pain and suffering, loss of amenities, future loss of earnings and expenses, and loss of earning capacity. This is not, however, an exhaustive list.

2.1.1 Damages for pain and suffering These cover past and future physical and mental pain and suffering resulting from the injuries and necessary treatment for them. Damages can also be awarded for nervous shock at learning of injuries to others (*McLoughlin* v *O'Brian* [1983] AC 410). The damages will take account of any suffering to the plaintiff resulting from the realisation (if any) of a reduced life expectancy (Administration of Justice Act 1982, s 1). Normally, one award of damages is made to cover this item and loss of amenities (but see 2.1.2).

The amounts awarded for pain and suffering and loss of amenity increase over the years as the value of money falls. For values of the pound sterling at various dates see *Kemp*, Appendix E. However, awards should not attempt to predict future inflation (*Wright* v

British Railways Board [1983] 2 AC 773). It is therefore important to use case law with caution, particularly since there are fewer reported cases on less serious injuries. However, refer to Kemp and Kemp, *The Quantum of Damages, Current Law, New Law Journal* or the Lexis file on quantum of damages in personal injuries cases. In larger cases which are likely to be litigated in the High Court it is advisable to seek counsel's opinion on quantum.

Some useful starting points are given by the figures suggested by the Criminal Injuries Compensation Board (1987) as follows:

	£
undisplaced nasal fracture	550
displaced nasal fracture	850
fractured jaw needing wiring	1750
simple fracture of tibia, fibula, ulna or radius with complete recovery	1750–2500
loss of two front upper teeth	1500
loss of vision in one eye	13,000
total loss of hearing in one ear	10,000
scar to face, unmarried man, 20	5000
scar to face, unmarried woman, 20	8000

The minimum claim that the Board will consider is for injuries justifying an award of £550.

Note also that awards over £80,000 for pain and suffering and loss of amenity are rare. See *Housecroft* v *Burnett* [1986] 1 All ER 332, CA.

2.1.2 Damages for loss of amenity This refers to the extent to which the injuries prevent the plaintiff taking part in pre-accident activities and will, therefore, be increased if the plaintiff had many sporting or other activities which can no longer be pursued. On this the prognosis section of the medical report will be vital.

This head of general damages is objective and can thus be awarded even though the plaintiff is unconscious and thus feels no pain, preventing damages for pain and suffering from being awarded (*Lim Poh Choò* v *Camden and Islington AHA* [1980] AC 174).

2.1.3 Future loss of earnings and expenses These often form the bulk of very large awards of damages. They are estimated by the trial judge who does the following calculation:

$$\text{multiplier} \times \text{multiplicand} = \text{product}$$

The *product* is a lump sum representing the current value of the plaintiff's future loss. In practice, this is taken as the amount needed to buy an annuity yielding the amount of the plaintiff's annual loss for the period fixed by the court (which because of the uncertainties of life is always less than the plaintiff's life expectancy).

The *multiplicand* represents the plaintiff's net annual loss of earnings and expenses at the date of trial, ie the estimated future rate of earnings net of tax, national insurance and work expenses (eg in travelling to work). Account must be taken of future job prospects (obtain a reference from the plaintiff's employers or teachers) and other factors (though not inflation) which would probably have increased the plaintiff's current loss of earnings and current expenses, and extra costs such as nursing care.

The *multiplier* is a conventional figure, fixed by the judge, related to the number of years the plaintiff would have worked but for the accident. It makes no difference that the plaintiff will not in fact live so long because the accident has shortened his or her life expectancy: a *living* plaintiff can recover damages for these 'lost years', although the plaintiff's estimated living expenses for those years must be deducted (*Pickett* v *British Rail Engineering* [1980] AC 136).

However, in fixing the multiplier, the judge takes a lower figure than the predicted pre-accident working life expectancy, because of the possibility that the plaintiff might have died or been made unemployed before the end of that period, and because the plaintiff is receiving the damages in a lump sum now rather than when they would have been earned. Indeed, the court will assume that the plaintiff will invest the damages and earn 4–5 per cent interest (*Auty* v *NCB* [1985] 1 WLR 784).

The following is a general guide to the appropriate multiplier:

Predicted working life (years)	Multiplier
5	5
10	8
15	11
20	13
25	15
30	16
35	17
40	18

The courts have disapproved of the use of higher, actuarially based multipliers.

2.1.4 Loss of earning capacity This covers the situation where instead of, or in addition to, any current loss of earnings, the plaintiff has been put at a disadvantage on the labour market by the injury

15

in that he or she may lose his job more readily than able-bodied employees, and if this happens, may find it harder to find another job or such a well-paid job. The leading case is *Smith* v *Manchester Corporation* [1974] 17 KIR 1, CA. The amount of such awards is always uncertain and can vary from a nominal amount to substantial awards of two years' loss of earnings or more, depending on the evidence.

2.2 Heads of special damage

These cover earnings already lost at the date of trial and expenses resulting from the accident which have already been incurred at that date.

2.2.1 Past lost earnings This covers the plaintiff's net loss (after making the necessary deductions: see 2.4) from the date of the accident to the date of the trial. In the usual case of a plaintiff in regular salaried employment it can be calculated by obtaining details of the plaintiff's earnings for the twenty-six weeks before the accident (to allow for variations due to illness, holidays etc) net of tax and national insurance, and multiplying this by the number of weeks off work. The plaintiff should add any pay rises, bonuses and commission which would have been earned. If the plaintiff is self-employed, the plaintiff's accounts for the last few years will be needed and expert evidence from accountants may be needed to establish the extent of the loss.

Loss of other fringe benefits such as free board and lodging or free use of a car should be added, as should loss of opportunities, eg of taking part in a professional sporting fixture (*Mulvaine* v *Joseph* (1968) 112 SJ 927).

2.2.2 Expenses incurred as a result of the accident These must be reasonable: the plaintiff must take reasonable steps to mitigate losses. But a wide variety of expenses may be claimable as follows:

- Travel to and from hospital and/or medical examinations.
- Medical treatment costs which include NHS charges, eg for prescriptions and spectacles, or the cost of private treatment since there is no obligation to use NHS facilities (Law Reform (Personal Injuries) Act 1948, s 2(4)).
- Special living accommodation or transport. Expert evidence will be needed. If the plaintiff thus acquires a capital asset, only the cost over and above what would have been incurred anyway can be claimed (*George* v *Pinnock* [1973] 1 WLR 118).

- Extra expenditure of a normal type, eg the extra cost of clothing and laundry incurred by a disabled plaintiff (*Povey* v *Governors of Rydal School* [1970] 1 All ER 841).
- Expenses in connection with the damaged vehicle, eg the loss of any no claims bonus, towing charges, any reduction in the value of the car despite repair, the cost of alternative transport either hired or public.
- Loss of clothing, crash helmet etc, although only the value at the time of the accident, after allowing for depreciation, can be claimed.
- Payments to other persons or expenses incurred by them on the plaintiff's behalf, eg payments to friends and relatives for helping to care for the plaintiff, or the expenses of such people visiting the plaintiff in hospital.

2.3   Interest on damages

2.3.1   Purpose of awarding interest   Interest is meant to compensate the plaintiff for having to wait for the money. Therefore, if the loss has not yet been incurred, no interest is claimable. The rules as to interest in non-fatal cases will be dealt with here and the rules in fatal cases are dealt with in 2.5 and 2.6.

2.3.2   Authority for awarding interest   Interest may be awarded in personal injury cases where the damages do not exceed £200, and, generally, must be awarded where they exceed £200, ie the great majority of cases (Supreme Court Act 1981, s 35A; County Courts Act 1984, s 69). These provisions apply both to final judgments concluding the case and to interlocutory judgments, such as judgment on liability with damages and interest to be assessed later. These provisions should be referred to when claiming interest in the indorsement of claim on the writ, and when pleading the claim for interest in the statement or particulars of claim (see Chapters 5 and 12).

2.3.3.   Guidelines on awarding interest   The 1981 and 1984 Acts leave the period and rate of interest at the discretion of the court. The courts have laid down the following guidelines to cover most cases, though the judge has a discretion not to follow them in appropriate cases. In particular, if one party is guilty of gross delay, the court may increase or reduce the interest rate and/or alter the period for which it is allowed (*Dexter* v *Courtaulds* [1984] 1 WLR 372). The guidelines are:

- Special damages carry interest at half the average of the special investment account rates for the period from the date of the accident to the date of the trial (*Pickett* v *British Rail Engineering* [1980] AC 136). The current special investment account rate is 12¼ per cent. For details of past rates see the table by RM Nelson-Jones (1987) *Law Society's Gazette* 2687.

• Damages for future loss of earnings and future expenses normally carry no interest since they have not yet been incurred.

• Damages for pain and suffering and loss of amenities normally carry interest at 2 per cent from the date of the service of the writ or summons to the date of the trial (*Wright* v *British Railways Board* [1983] 2 All ER 698, HL).

2.4 Deductions in calculating damages

The following will need to be considered in order to prevent the plaintiff from being over-compensated for the losses.

2.4.1 Income tax and other deductions from earnings Damages and interest for personal injuries are not taxable when received by the plaintiff. Accordingly, income tax at the highest rate applicable to the plaintiff is deducted when calculating the past and future loss of earnings (*BTC* v *Gourley* [1956] AC 185). Further, the plaintiff must give credit for income tax rebates and the receipt of a tax 'holiday', ie non-payment of tax for a period on the plaintiff's return to work (*Brayson* v *Willmott-Breedon* (1976) *Kemp and Kemp* 9–010.). Obtain the details from the Inland Revenue with the plaintiff's written consent.

National insurance contributions must also be deducted, as must compulsory superannuation contributions (although the loss of pension rights can be claimed for) (*Dews* v *NCB* [1986] 3 WLR 227).

2.4.2 Payments from the plaintiff's employer Statutory sick pay is now payable by the employer for the first twenty-eight weeks off work (first eight weeks 1983–April 1986). It is deductible in full (*Palfrey* v *GLC* [1985] ICR 437). Further payments by employers will be deductible in full if they are made as of right, even if they are in fact met from an insurance policy paid for by the employer (*Hussain* v *New Taplow Paper Mills Ltd* [1988] 2 WLR 266, HL). However, they are not deductible if made as discretionary payments or only on condition that the plaintiff seeks recovery of them from the defendant. Accordingly, the plaintiff's contract of employment should be checked and the employer contacted in case of doubt.

2.4.3 Partially deductible state benefits Half the following benefits received by the plaintiff for the five years from the date of the accident are deductible under the Law Reform (Personal Injuries) Act 1948, s 2(1):

- Sickness benefit.
- Invalidity benefit.
- Non-contributory invalidity benefit.
- Injury benefit (now abolished).
- Disablement benefit.

The DHSS will supply details of such benefits paid on written request referring to s 2(1). Benefits received after the five-year period are not deductible at all (*Denman* v *Essex AHA* [1984] QB 735).

2.4.4 Fully deductible state benefits For state benefits not listed in the 1948 Act, the courts are increasingly requiring full deduction, for example:

- Unemployment benefit (*Nabi* v *British Leyland (UK)* [1980] 1 WLR 529).
- Redundancy pay (*Colledge* v *Bass Mitchells* (1987) *The Independent* 14 December).
- Supplementary benefit if already received (*Lincoln* v *Hayman* [1982] 1 WLR 488) (and presumably now income support).
- Family income supplement (*Gaskill* v *Preston* [1981] 3 All ER 427) (and presumably now family credit).

The plaintiff must also give credit for savings, eg in lighting and heating the home, resulting from being maintained at the public expense while receiving NHS treatment (Administration of Justice Act 1982, s 5).

2.4.5 Non-deductible state benefits

- Attendance allowance, mobility allowance (*Bowker* v *Rose* (1978) 122 SJ 147).
- Redundancy pay unless relating to incapacity resulting from the accident (*Mills* v *Hassal* [1983] ICR 330).
- Retirement pension (*Hewson* v *Downs* [1970] 1 QB 73).

2.4.6 Other benefits received Other benefits received by the plaintiff as a result of the accident, eg gifts and charitable payments, payments under insurance policies and private health care schemes such as BUPA are not deductible at all.

2.5 Fatal cases: Law Reform (Miscellaneous Provisions) Act 1934

The plaintiff's estate can recover reasonable funeral expenses, any special damages the plaintiff could have claimed including loss of earnings (if any) from the date of the accident to the date of death, and general damages for pain, suffering and loss of amenity (unless death was instantaneous). However, damages for loss of earnings in the 'lost years' (see 2.3) cannot be claimed (Administration of Justice Act 1982, s 4).

2.6 Fatal cases: Fatal Accidents Act 1976.

The following types of damages may be claimed.

2.6.1 Damages for bereavement These are currently £3500 and can be claimed by the spouse of the deceased, or the parents of a deceased unmarried minor (Administration of Justice Act 1982, s 1A). This is the only non-financial loss that can be claimed.

2.6.2 Loss of dependency on the deceased This applies where the deceased contributed to the financial support of the claimants. It covers, firstly, the claimants' actual loss to the date of the trial. If the deceased was a minor this may be little or nothing. Secondly, there can be claimed the estimated future loss. This could be considerable if the deceased was a child to whom the claimants would later have looked for support.

In fixing the appropriate *multiplier* to reflect the length of the dependency, the court will have regard to the probable working life of the deceased, but will normally reduce this figure considerably to take account of such factors as age, the hazards of the deceased's life, the dependants' expectation of life and, in the case of dependants who are widowers or unmarried minors, their prospects of re-marriage. The multiplier is taken as at the time of the deceased's death, not the date of trial, but the number of years for which special damages have been awarded is deducted (*Graham* v *Dodds* [1983] 1 WLR 808).

In calculating the *multiplicand*, the annual net loss, where the deceased was the main breadwinner, it is usually simplest to take the deceased's net income and deduct a figure to cover the money the deceased spent on him or herself. This will usually be taken as about 33 per cent (ie 66 per cent dependency) if there are no children or 25 per cent (ie 75 per cent dependency) if there are children (*Harris* v *Empress Motors* [1983] 3 All ER 561). If the deceased was not the main earner, then it is necessary to calculate the net annual loss, taking account of the loss of the deceased's earnings and the cost of providing substitute services, but deducting any financial savings in the cost of food, clothing etc (*Spittle* v *Bunney* (1988) *The Independent* 10 February). However, any benefits accruing to the dependants from the deceased's estate are disregarded.

2.6.3   Interest   Damages from the date of death to the date of the trial carry interest at half the average special investment account rate during that period. Damages for future loss from the date of the trial carry no interest.

Such damages will be apportioned by the court between the dependants, generally giving the widow the largest share and younger children more than older children. Damages for pain and suffering awarded under the 1934 Act are deducted from the 1976 Act award.

2.7   Provisional damages

2.7.1   Purpose of provisional damages   Normally only one award of damages can be made. If the plaintiff's condition later changes, he or she may turn out to have been under (or over) compensated. The court will try to take account of such possibilities in fixing its award but often the parties will seek to delay settling the case until the prognosis is clear. Other procedures for reducing delay in providing compensation for the plaintiff include interim payments of damages (see 6.3) and trying the issues of liability and quantum separately (see 7.1.2). The new provisional damages procedure is designed to deal with situations where there is a chance that the plaintiff will develop some *serious* disease or suffer some *serious* deterioration in physical or mental condition (Supreme Court Act 1981, s 32A).

2.7.2   When are provisional damages appropriate?   The reference to 'a chance' in s 32A implies that something less than the balance of probabilities is sufficient. Most head injuries, for example, carry some risk of epilepsy, clearly a serious deterioration. However, by February 1988 Lexis recorded only seven cases where provisional damages had been awarded. These included epilepsy risks and the risk of tetraplegia if the plaintiff suffered any further spinal injury. It seems that both plaintiffs' solicitors, and defendants' prefer a once and for all settlement. However, the plaintiff's solicitors should at least ask their consultant doctor whether a claim for provisional damages is advisable, since they must plead provisional damages if they later wish to claim them.

2.7.3 Provisional damages procedure (RSC Ord 37, r8)

1 Plaintiff specifically pleads provisional damages.
2 (No judgment in default can now be entered.)
   (Defendant may request further and better particulars of possible deterioration.)
   (Defendant may make written offer to submit to an award of provisional damages—similar in effect to a payment into court.)
3 Court makes order for provisional damages after trial or consent summons.
   (Possible deterioration/disease and period for application for further award usually stated.)
4 Plaintiff lodges medical report and other documents at court.
5 (Plaintiff within period gives three months' notice to defendant and defendant's insurers of intention to seek further award/extension of period and within twenty-one days of end of three months issues and serves summons for directions.)
   (Court preserves file for period. See [1985] 1 WLR 961.).
6 Directions complied with.
7 Court grants/refuses further award.

2.8 Damages payable by instalments

2.8.1 Purpose of the scheme Damages awarded by the court are payable immediately. However, it may be beneficial to the plaintiff, particularly one who is severely disabled, say, to receive payment by instalments. Previously, this was effectively prevented by the view of the Inland Revenue that such payments would incur liability to income tax. However, a new (voluntary) scheme which seems to prevent liability to income tax has just been agreed on an extra-statutory basis between the Revenue and the Association of British Insurers on the basis that the claim is being satisfied by periodic payments in lieu of a lump sum.

2.8.2 Structured settlements The 'structured settlement' is a financial package designed to meet the claimant's particular needs by way of periodical payments. These may be of a fixed amount or (probably more often) an amount linked to the retail prices index. They may be for a fixed term or (probably more often) for the rest of the plaintiff's life. The payments are in fact met by an annuity bought from a life office by the defendant's insurers. In addition, there will usually be a capital sum to cover expenses already incurred and wages already lost. A consent order should be obtained containing these terms. Where the plaintiff is a minor or incapable of managing his affairs the court's approval to the proposed settlement will still be needed in the usual way (see 9.2).

Schemes varying from the above pattern will need the specific approval of the Revenue if income tax liability is to be avoided.

2.8.3   When should structured settlements be used? The scheme has only recently been promoted by the ABI and currently is only likely to be suggested by defendants' insurers for claims of £250,000 or more. However, smaller claims may well be found to be suitable in due course. For further details see (1987) NLJ 926 or (1987) SJ 1678.

2.9   Common problems and their solutions

Problem	Solution
Defendant's insurers claim plaintiff will recover once claim concluded.	Get psychiatrist's report on whether plaintiff has a genuine claim of neurosis arising from the accident which will increase the damages.
Defendant's insurers claim female plaintiff would have married and stopped work.	Claim damages for reduced prospects of marriage if appropriate.
Defendant's insurers refuse to pay full cost of repairs to vehicle on the grounds there is an element of 'betterment'.	Obtain report on value before accident and after repairs; cost of repairs may, in fact, not greatly increase current value over pre-accident value.
Defendant's insurers refuse to pay interest.	Threaten and, if necessary, take proceedings solely to recover the interest.
Plaintiff claims damages for trifling injuries apparently to take the claim over £500 in order to recover costs (see 3.2.8).	Require satisfactory medical evidence; threaten and, if necessary, apply to strike out the claim for personal injury damages (see 3.2.8).

Plaintiff claims substantial loss of future earnings based on future promotion or career prospects.

Plaintiff claims provisional damages.

Require strict proof from current employers, school, college, careers adviser.

Serve request for further and better particulars of deterioration or disease alleged and the time within which it may occur. Ask the judge to specify the conditions for which a further award may be claimed and a period for such a claim.

CHAPTER 3
FINANCING THE CASE

3.1 General principles

You should consider at the outset how the litigation will be financed. This necessarily entails an understanding of the general principles as to the award of costs, and of legal aid and its alternatives.

Only an outline of the basic rules is given here. For more detail on costs see Rigby, *Contentious Costs* or *Longman's Costs and Fees Service*.

3.2 Liability for costs between the parties

3.2.1 The court's discretion The award of costs is within the discretion of the court (RSC Ord 62, r 2; CCR Ord 38, r 1). However, this discretion must be used judicially. Normally, the loser will be ordered to pay the costs of the winner, although in some cases these will not be the costs of the whole proceedings. Examples include where the plaintiff fails at the trial to recover more in damages than the amount paid into court by the defendant (see 3.2.4); where the defendant has succeeded in an interlocutory application for which costs have been awarded; and where the defendant has succeeded in some other aspect of the case, such as a counterclaim, for which costs have been awarded. Note that an order for costs must be made if it is sought to hold the other side to payment.

3.2.2 The amount of costs The amount of costs payable by one party to another are limited to the *costs of the action* (*In Re Gibson's Settlement Trusts* [1981] Ch 179) and these will not include all the work done for the client, eg work done in order to have a limitation on a legal aid certificate removed. The basis on which costs between the parties is ordered is the *standard basis* ie a reasonable amount in respect of all costs reasonably incurred, the benefit of the doubt on questions of reasonableness being given to the paying and not the receiving party (RSC Ord 62, r 12; CCR Ord 38, r 19A). The more generous *indemnity basis* will only be awarded in exceptional cases, eg where the court disapproves strongly of the way the paying party has conducted the case. Under this basis, the receiving party receives the benefit of any doubt on questions of reasonableness.

3.2.3 Interlocutory applications These are applications to the court made after the proceedings have begun and before final judgment. In a routine case the usual order will be *costs in the cause*, ie the recipient of the costs of that application will be the party who wins the trial. However, where the application has been made necessary by the unreasonable attitude of the other side in, eg, not giving proper discovery or adequate particulars of a pleading, then the solicitor should ask the court to award costs to the client *in any event*.

Note also that the costs of instructing counsel on an interlocutory application cannot be awarded unless a certificate that the matter was fit for counsel is obtained.

3.2.4 Payments into court and written offers These are two procedures defendants can use in order to put pressure on plaintiffs or third parties to settle the claim. If the plaintiff rejects a payment into court and at the trial recovers less than or the same amount as that paid into court after deducting contributory negligence and ignoring interest accruing after payment in, then costs will be recovered from the defendant up to the time the notice of payment into court was received, but not later costs; indeed, the plaintiff will be liable to pay the defendant's costs incurred after that date. The defendant can set off these costs against the damages to be paid to the plaintiff.

Written offers are letters making proposals for settlement which are expressed to be made without prejudice, save that the right is reserved to draw them to the attention of the court on the question of costs. They may be made by a defendant or third party or by a co-defendant with regard to their share of the damages that will be paid to the plaintiff (RSC Ord 16, r 10; CCR Ord 12, r 7). Where there are split trials (in the High Court) a party can make an offer to accept liability up to a specified proportion of the amount fixed by the court (RSC Ord 33, r 4A). Finally, in the High Court a defendant may offer to submit to an award of provisional damages (RSC Ord 37, r 9). There is also a general right to make written offers where a payment into court is not feasible: (RSC Ord 22, r 14).

3.2.5 Where there are several plaintiffs or defendants Two or more successful plaintiffs with the same interest will normally recover only the costs of one set of solicitors and counsel unless the court thinks separate representation was justified. If the plaintiffs fail, then the court will apportion their liability for the defendant's costs.

Co-defendants may be separately represented, but the extra costs will only be allowed if the court thinks separate representation was required (*Harbin* v *Masterman* [1896] 1 Ch 351). When the plaintiff has reasonably joined in several defendants, costs are allowed against them all if the plaintiff succeeds against them all. If the plaintiff succeeds against only some, he or she will generally have to pay the costs of the successful defendant, but they can be recovered from the unsuccessful defendant (*Bullock* v *London General Omnibus Co* [1907] 1 KB 264). However, if the plaintiff is on legal aid or is of limited means, the losing defendant may be ordered to pay the costs of the successful defendant direct (*Sanderson* v *Blyth Theatre Co* [1903] 2 KB 533).

3.2.6   Costs against the solicitor   Note that the court has the power to award costs against the party's solicitor who is guilty of misconduct or neglect in the conduct of the proceedings.

Alternatively, or in addition, it can order the solicitor's bill to be disallowed in whole or part (RSC Ord 62, r 28; CCR Ord 38, r 19A).

3.2.7   Types of costs in personal injury cases

- Taxed costs. These are scrutinised and approved by the court. This will be the usual position in personal injury cases in the absence of agreement.
- Agreed costs. It is desirable for the parties to agree costs to save the expense of a taxation. Most insurers will be reasonable about this.
- Costs assessed by the Legal Aid Board. This is normally only possible where the case has been concluded without an order for costs being made and the amount claimed does not exceed £500.
- Costs assessed by the court. The judge can be asked to assess costs at the trial. This saves the expense of a taxation but the amounts awarded are low.
- Costs fixed by CCR Appendix B. These will be all the costs recoverable if judgment is entered without trial in a county court action solely to recover the cost of repairs to a vehicle arising out of a road accident since this is treated as a liquidated claim (CCR Ord 1, r 10).

3.2.8   County court variations   In the county court the amount of costs recoverable will depend on the scale applicable. If the plaintiff wins, the scale will be fixed by the amount recovered; if the defendant wins, by the amount claimed (CCR Ord 38, rr 3, 4). Accordingly, the plaintiff, by limiting the claim to the maximum amount which can realistically be recovered, can reduce any potential liability for the defendant's costs should the defendant win. The scales are:

Sum of money	Scale applicable
£	
Exceeding 25 but not exceeding 100	lower scale
Exceeding 100 but not exceeding 500	scale 1
Exceeding 500 but not exceeding 3,000	scale 2
Exceeding 3000 but not exceeding 5,000	scale 3

However, it is worth asking the registrar to use his or her discretion to exceed the scale maxima for particular items (eg for expert witness fees and expenses) in suitable cases.

Claims not exceeding £500 will normally be referred to arbitration once a defence has been filed. In arbitrations under CCR Ord 19, r 2 only very limited costs are allowed. However, it should be possible in a personal injury action for the reference to arbitration to be rescinded so that the action is tried in the usual way (*Pepper* v *Healey* [1982] RTR 411, CA). Costs will then be available. If the action is not defended and the defendants make a payment into court, the plaintiff is entitled to continue with the action to recover costs (*Smith* v *Springer* [1987] 3 All ER 252, CA).

3.3 Costs between solicitor and client

3.3.1 Liability for costs The client, unless in receipt of legal advice and assistance or legal aid, is, of course, contractually bound to pay the solicitor's proper costs, whether or not the solicitor wins the case and whether or not an order for costs is obtained against the opponent. Further, it is not possible to agree to be paid a proportion of any damages recovered since this would amount to a contingency fee (Solicitors' Practice Rules 1987, r 8). The client's liability is to pay *solicitor and client costs*. It is for the client to show that items or amounts claimed are unreasonable, and unusual steps will be deemed reasonable if the client approved them. The solicitor should, therefore, seek the client's written approval for major items of expenditure and warn the client in the case of unusual items (eg a road accident simulation by a consulting automobile engineer) that the cost may not be recovered from the opponent.

3.3.2 Duties to the client Under the Law Society's general standard on information on costs for the individual client (see *The*

Professional Conduct of Solicitors, Appendix C7) the solicitor should inform the client as accurately as possible of the likely cost before starting proceedings, giving warning of the difficulties of doing this and explaining when and what items of expenditure are likely to arise. The solicitor should also regularly report the costs position to the client, who should be told that a limit may be imposed on the costs to be incurred on his or her behalf. Finally, it should be pointed out not only that if the case is lost, the client is likely to have to pay the other side's costs, but also that even if the case is won, the solicitor will be charging solicitor and client costs yet is likely to recover only standard basis costs from the other side.

3.3.3   Easing cash flow   In the absence of contrary agreement, a personal injury action is an entire contract for which the solicitor can only charge when the matter is complete. As this may take several years, it is advisable at the very least to ask the client for funds on account of costs (Solicitors Act 1974, s 65(2)) to meet the very substantial disbursements involved, eg for experts' reports. If the action is going to be a protracted one it is advisable to agree to submit interim bills.

3.4   The Green Form and 'ALAS' schemes

See the Legal Aid Act 1988 and regulations made thereunder.

Remember that the solicitor should advise the client about eligibility for both the Green Form and legal aid schemes. Failure to do so is likely to be both professional misconduct and negligence.

3.4.1   The legal advice and assistance scheme   The client should, if within the financial limits (indicated by the current 'key card') sign a 'green form' under this scheme at the first interview. The scheme enables the solicitor, provided the client is within the scheme's financial limits, to advise and assist the client but it cannot be used to take any steps in court proceedings, although it could be used to advise a party on how to draft pleadings etc in a claim not exceeding £500 which, exceptionally, is going to be arbitrated rather than tried.

However, the scheme can cover not only oral and written advice and negotiations with insurers but also obtaining reports, eg the police report or instructing counsel to advise, eg on liability and/or quantum. Such steps will almost certainly involve seeking an extension of the £50 limit of expenditure. This should be done by submitting form LA/Rep/6A Ext to the Board Area Office *before* the limit is reached, since any extension will not be retrospective, stating the new expenditure limit sought and the reasons why the extension is needed. Note that if the plaintiff can already show a prima facie case the application will be refused since a legal aid certificate should be applied for.

3.4.2 The 'ALAS' scheme This scheme has been designed by the Law Society to promote greater public awareness of their rights in personal injury cases. It is operated by many but not all firms. Under the scheme the solicitor provides a free first interview at which the client is given advice on the merits of the claim and the likely cost of pursuing it.

3.5 Legal aid

3.5.1 Applying for legal aid If the client is likely to be financially eligible, it is normally advisable to apply for legal aid as soon as possible, particularly given the long delays in processing applications by those not on social security. However, it is important that the application form (Form A1, Application—General) is properly filled in. In particular, the application should be made as strong as possible by enclosing a full client's statement, any police or other accident report, and statements from any witnesses. (But do not delay sending in the form until all these are to hand.) The extent of the injuries and their effect on the plaintiff should be brought out since the Legal Aid Board will not normally grant legal aid if the claim is worth no more than £500. Similarly, there may be difficulties if in a non-road accident claim the defendant is uninsured since he or she may well have no means to pay any damages awarded.

Note that where there are several possible plaintiffs it is not normally possible to select the poorest as the applicant for legal aid in order to fund a 'test' case with the least expense to the potential claimants. In such cases the Legal Aid Board may well assume that the potential plaintiffs can contribute towards the costs of representation. However, the Board may be prepared to allocate representation in such 'class' claims to a limited number of firms under the Legal Aid Act 1988.

3.5.2 Scope of legal aid If legal aid is granted, or offered subject to payment of a contribution, the scope of the certificate or offer should be carefully checked and any conditions and limitations explained to the client. Limited certificates are often granted in personal injury cases. Common limitations are that the certificate is only for the purpose of obtaining counsel's opinion; that it goes up to and including discovery; or that it extends to all steps up to setting the action down for trial. Normally a satisfactory counsel's opinion will be needed for such limitations to be removed (although see now the Legal Aid Regulations 1988).

Even if the certificate is a full one, ensure that it covers what the client needs to do, eg it covers any counterclaim as well as the defence. If the solicitor wishes to join in another party the certificate will have to be amended. Further, it is advisable to obtain the Legal Aid Board's approval (and the client's) before taking any unusual step, incurring any unusual expenditure, or obtaining an expert's report (at any rate beyond the first medical report). Such authority will prevent the costs involved being later disallowed on taxation of the legal aid bill.

3.5.3 Duties under the scheme   The client must, if liable, now pay contributions throughout the duration of the case under the Legal Aid Act 1988. The client must also inform the Legal Aid Board of any change in his or her means. Eligibility for legal aid may then be re-assessed. This will be important if the client is awarded a large payment of interim damages.

The assisted person's solicitor also has duties to the Legal Aid Fund, the court and, to a very limited extent, the other side. The Legal Aid Board must be kept informed of any changes in the client's means, of the progress of the case and, in particular, if the client wishes to pursue a course the solicitor considers an abuse of the scheme. An example of this would be where the client refuses a payment into court against the solicitor's and counsel's advice. In these circumstances, the Board may then discharge the certificate. Further, the solicitor must lodge the original certificate at court and give notice of issue of the certificate to all parties (although the notice need not disclose any financial conditions).

Finally, should the assisted person's opponent consider that the assisted person is abusing the scheme the opponent can make representations to the Board who may decide to discharge the certificate. It is also possible to make representations before the certificate is granted.

3.5.4 Payment under the legal aid certificate   (Except where the Legal Aid Board assesses the bill (see 3.2.7.)

1 At trial seek order for Legal Aid Act taxation (standard basis).
2 Prepare bill for taxation.
3 Lodge bill at court within three months of end of case (with receipts and file).

4 Taxation hearing or provisional taxation.

5 Send allocatur with report on case, damages and costs recovered, and client's authority to discharge the certificate to Legal Aid Board.

6 (Ask Board to allow you to release balance of damages to client on your undertaking that your costs will not exceed sum retained to meet statutory charge.)

7 Legal Aid Board pays your bill.

8 Board reimburses itself from any costs recovered from opponent, any client contribution and, if necessary, from the damages under the statutory charge.

9 Board discharges client's certificate and sends client balance of damages and any contribution on any money recovered. The client must be warned that even if he wins he may not receive all the damages.

If he loses, the client will only be liable to pay the opponent those costs which the court thinks reasonable in all the circumstances, including the means of the parties and their conduct of the case (Legal Aid Act 1988, ss 11, 14). In practice, a reasonable amount is often taken as being the amount the assisted person is liable to contribute (if any) under the legal aid certificate. A non-legally aided party can therefore be heavily penalised since a legally aided person may be beaten yet only be liable for little or nothing in the way of costs.

However, if the non-legally aided person is the *defendant* he or she may seek an order for costs against the Legal Aid Fund: Legal Aid Act 1988, ss 12, 16. The non-legally aided person must show that otherwise he or she will suffer severe financial hardship. While the applicant does not need to show that otherwise he or she will suffer penury, it is highly unlikely that insured or large corporate defendants will be able to satisfy this condition (*Hanning* v *Maitland* [1970] 1 QB 580).

Finally, note the following means of helping the solicitor's cash flow:

• Submit green forms for payment as soon as the legal aid certificate is issued.

• Submit periodic claims for payment on account of disbursements (minimum £30) to cover experts' fees, court fees etc. This can be done *in advance* of the payment being made.

• Seek a payment on account of profit costs. See (1988) 16 *Law Society's Gazette*, 18.

3.6   Alternatives to legal aid

3.6.1   Legal expenses insurance   Your client may have a specific legal expenses policy. More likely, the client will have cover under a more general policy such as house contents, a motor policy or a small boat or pet insurance policy. The insurers may, however, have the right to nominate solicitors to deal with claims covered by the policy: check the wording of the particular policy.

3.6.2   Trades unions   These may well provide legal assistance for industrial injury claims, again normally conditional on using a particular firm of solicitors.

3.6.3   Social security benefits   The solicitor should check that a client in urgent financial need is receiving all the social security benefits to which he or she is entitled.

If the plaintiff is still off work after twenty-eight weeks, then provided sufficient contributions have been made, he or she will be eligible for sickness benefit or invalidity benefit in long-term cases. Victims of industrial accidents may be able to obtain disablement pension and in some cases reduced earnings allowance if they are at least 14 per cent disabled and, if the disablement is 100 per cent, constant attendance or exceptionally severe disablement allowance. These benefits are on top of any other social security benefits they may be receiving.

This will also provide a quick and relatively expert opinion on the extent to which the plaintiff is disabled and whether any such disability was attributable to the accident. The decision letter should be obtained from the DHSS and if disablement pension is refused, consideration should be given to an appeal.

Plaintiffs in non-industrial accidents who have made insufficient contributions to be eligible for sickness or invalidity benefit may be entitled to income support (formerly supplementary benefit) under the Social Security Act 1986.

Plaintiffs who have returned to work but perhaps at considerably less pay, for example because they can only work reduced hours, may be eligible for family credit (replacing family income supplement) if the claimant or his or her partner is engaged on average for at least twenty-four hours paid work per week and has care of a child (Social Security Act 1986).

For further details, see Pollard, *Social Welfare Law*.

3.6.4   Interim payments   Although these are discussed in detail at 6.3, it is worth considering applying for an interim payment at the outset of any case where there are substantial injuries and which seem strong on liability. If legal aid is granted, such a payment is exempt from the Legal Aid Board charge, and nor will it cause the client's eligibility for legal aid to be re-assessed. If, however, there is no legal aid, the payment can be used to fund the running of the case.

3.7 Costs and the MIB and CICB.

3.7.1 The Motor Insurers' Bureau The MIB will pay reasonable costs under the uninsured driver scheme but only £110 profit costs plus VAT and reasonable disbursements, plus a further 30 per cent of £110 for each extra claimant, under the untraced driver scheme.

3.7.2 The Criminal Injuries Compensation Board The Board will not pay applicants' legal costs, but may pay the expenses of the applicant and any witnesses.

3.8 Common problems and their solutions

Problem	Solution
Client refused legal aid.	Obtain further evidence, after extension to green form if needed. Appeal against refusal on merits. If refused on financial grounds re-apply if client's means change.
Opponent granted legal aid.	Require notice of any limitations on the certificate other than financial conditions. Make representations to the Legal Aid Board if you think abuse of the scheme will occur or has occurred.
Substantial amount taxed off bill.	Apply for reconsideration of the bill specifying the items complained about. If still dissatisfied seek a review by the judge. (Note that leave of the Legal Aid Board needed in legal aid cases).

Insurers offer to pay a claim not exceeding £500 in full but refuse to pay costs on the ground it would have been arbitrated.

Threaten/continue with the claim if for unliquidated damages; until damages assessed impossible to know the amount of damages or costs (*Smith* v *Springer* [1987] 3 All ER 252, CA).

CHAPTER 4

INVESTIGATING THE CLAIM

This chapter will consider the basic practical steps which will be needed in every personal injury action, up to the stage of deciding to take court proceedings. Some cases will, of course, never go further than this (see Chapter 10).

For more detail see Pritchard, *Personal Injury Litigation*, Chapter 4.

4.1 Taking instructions

The following vital matters should be attended to at the first meeting with the client.

4.1.1 Conflicts of interest Check that neither you nor a colleague have been instructed by anyone with an actual or probable conflicting interest in the matter. Otherwise you may disqualify your firm from acting for either party.

4.1.2 Financing the case Conduct the first interview under the ALAS scheme if appropriate, or under the Green Form scheme. Prepare and lodge the application for legal aid, where appropriate, as soon as possible; further information can always be sent in later. Advise the client generally as to liability for both his or her own and the opponent's costs. See generally Chapter 3.

4.1.3 The client's statement Allow the client to tell the basic story in his or her own words at the first meeting. However, once the client is at ease and you understand the basic history, you need full details of:

● Pre-accident work, state of health and lifestyle.
● What the client remembers of the accident, details of any witnesses and whether the accident was reported to the police or Health and Safety Executive.
● Details of the injuries and treatment.
● The consequences in terms of time off work, expenses and benefits received, and effect on the client's leisure activities.

Do not worry if some information would be inadmissible in court, but do ensure that the client reads the statement and signs and dates it. This will protect you if the client later changes the story; further, if the client dies or becomes unable to give evidence before the trial, the statement can still go into evidence under the Civil Evidence Act 1968 (see 8.3).

4.1.4   Initial advice   It should be possible in many cases to give the client some idea of the chances of success on liability at the first interview or soon afterwards. It is generally wise, however, to defer any definite advice on the value of the claim until a medical report and information on special damages has been obtained.

4.2   Preliminary correspondence

4.2.1   Contacting witnesses   Interview witnesses and take signed and dated statements from them for the reasons set out above. There is nothing to stop you interviewing someone who has already given a statement to another party: there is no property in a witness. Although other employees, say, may be reluctant to give evidence against the employer, you can remind them that you can, if necessary, compel them to attend court to give evidence (8.3.2).

4.2.2   Obtaining reports   If the accident happened on a public road, it should have been reported to the police. The police report will normally be available from the chief constable once any criminal proceedings are completed or the police have decided not to prosecute. For details of the current fees see 10.4. The report will contain details of the vehicles, parties and their insurers, the accident scene, a plan and sometimes photographs, the views of the investigating officer as to the cause of the accident and, often, statements by those involved and any witnesses. If the case becomes defended it is possible to take further statements from the investigating officer on payment of a further fee and submitting the statement to the police for checking.

In the case of industrial accidents, ask to see the employer's accident book and in the case of major incidents, ask the Health and Safety Executive whether the notification form (Form 2058) has been submitted, and if they can release any statements or photographs.

It may also be advisable to instruct expert witnesses at this stage: see 4.4 below.

4.2.3 Details of special damages It will be necessary to write to the plaintiff's employers for details of pre- and post-accident earnings and of any statutory sick pay received; to the DHSS for details of any sickness or other state benefits received (referring to Law Reform (Personal Injuries) Act 1948, s 2); and to the plaintiff's tax office for confirmation of any tax rebates paid.

4.2.4 The letter before action Once the plaintiff's solicitor is satisfied that the plaintiff has a cause of action, the solicitor should write formally to the defendant (or the defendant's solicitor, if known to have been instructed) indicating the grounds of the claim, the nature, in broad terms, of the damage alleged, and that proceedings will be taken in the absence of a satisfactory settlement. If written to the defendant, the letter should also ask the defendant to refer the matter to his or her insurers. If written to the insurers, it is convenient for the plaintiff also to give formal notice of intended proceedings for the purpose of Road Traffic Act 1972, s 149 (see 1.2.2).

The letter should not be headed 'without prejudice', nor should it go into too much detail since otherwise the defendant may be able to suggest at the trial that the plaintiff has changed the story. On the other hand, failure by the plaintiff to give the defendant a chance to settle the claim might well lead the plaintiff to be deprived of costs in the proceedings which would have been unnecessary.

4.3 Other preliminary steps

4.3.1 Inspecting the accident scene It is useful for the lawyers involved to have familiarised themselves with the accident site (the 'locus in quo') and for photographs and a plan to be drawn up as soon as possible after the accident to capture important features such as skid marks. These should be agreed, if possible, in order that they may be put in evidence at any trial without difficulty.

In factory cases the inspection will normally be in the company of the expert(s) instructed by one or both parties. In this case it is important to ensure that the inspection keeps to the fact-finding role and does not broaden out into an informal 'arbitration' as to who was to blame.

In factory cases too, the defendant or the defendant's insurers may be reluctant to allow an inspection. In this case, the plaintiff's solicitors should threaten, and, if necessary apply, to the court under Supreme Court Act 1981, s 33 (1) or County Courts Act 1984, s 52 for an order for inspecting, photographing, preserving, sampling or experimenting with any property which may become involved in later proceedings, eg the machine alleged to have caused the injuries. The procedure is by way of originating summons (RSC Ord 29, r 7A: Oyez form S35) or originating application (CCR Ord 13, r 7: Oyez form N393) in the county court. For fees see Chapter 11. In each case an affidavit will be needed describing the property and the reasons for thinking that it will be involved in the forthcoming litigation. The court is likely to grant the application but award costs to the defendant.

4.3.2   Pre-action disclosure of documents   Again in factory cases, the defendant may have documents, such as safety committee minutes, relating to both the present and perhaps previous similar accidents that may indicate, for example, an unsafe system of work. The defendant may refuse to disclose whether there are such documents until the normal discovery stage after the case has begun. The plaintiff may under Supreme Court Act 1981, s 33(2) or County Courts Act 1984, s 52 apply to the court for an order that the defendant disclose whether there are documents relevant to a likely issue and, if so, to produce them to the plaintiff.

The procedure is governed by RSC Ord 24, r 7A and CCR Ord 13, r 7 and is similar to that for pre-action inspection of property. The plaintiff will normally be awarded an order for disclosure of specified documents if some basis of a case can be shown, but not if he or she is merely 'fishing' for evidence with no real reason for thinking there are grounds for holding the defendant liable.

4.3.3   Attending other proceedings   It is important to ascertain the outcome of any criminal proceedings (such as careless driving or breaches of health and safety regulations) against one or both of the parties since relevant convictions may be admissible in the civil proceedings (see Chapter 8). Further, attendance at such proceedings, and at proceedings such as inquests which have no formal effect on civil proceedings, may give an early idea of the available evidence.

4.4   Instructing expert witnesses

4.4.1   Preliminary matters   An expert medical report will be needed in all personal injury cases. A report from a consulting engineer will be needed in most industrial accident claims and in some road accident cases, although the services of an expert in road accident reconstructions are expensive and the cost may not always be recoverable from the defendant.

Apart from the first medical report, which will normally be recoverable without difficulty under the legal aid certificate, it is advisable to obtain the prior authority of the Legal Aid Board before instructing an expert, and they will normally set a limit on the fee payable. Accordingly, it is wise to check with the expert on the likely amount of the fee. You should also obtain the client's express authority to instruct the expert, in both private and legal aid cases, warning (the client) where appropriate that the cost may not be recoverable from the defendant.

4.4.2 Instructing doctors In all but the most trivial cases a report from a consultant rather than the plaintiff's general practitioner will be needed. In most cases, where limbs have been broken, the basic report should be from an orthopaedic surgeon. More specialised reports may also be needed, for example from a neuro-surgeon and possibly a clinical psychologist where brain damage is suspected, or from a psychiatrist where personality change is alleged.

Care should be taken to instruct a consultant who is reasonably sympathetic to the client's case, and understands the demands of a forensic medical report. The doctor in charge of the plaintiff's care may be familiar with his condition, but may sometimes be understandably optimistic about the prognosis. In practice, you can find out by consulting experienced colleagues that certain doctors are more sympathetic to plaintiffs or defendants respectively. In medical negligence cases, the Association of Victims of Medical Accidents can help find consultants willing to advise (for address, see 10.5).

When instructing the doctor, describe the basic history of the accident and enclose the client's statement, in the case of the plaintiff informing the doctor of the plaintiff's pre- and post-accident lifestyle. Also ask the doctor to consider whether the case would be suitable for an award of provisional damages if there is any real risk that the plaintiff's condition may seriously worsen later. Finally, enclose the plaintiff's consent for the hospital to disclose their records.

On receiving the report, go through it carefully with the client, unless the doctor has said that any parts of it are not to be communicated to the client. The following terms are commonly found in reports (for more detail see, eg the *Longman Medical Dictionary* and the diagrams in Pritchard, *Personal Injury Litigation*, Appendix J):

Abduction: moving a limb away from the medial line.
Adduction: moving a limb towards the medial line.
Ataxia: loss of control of movement due to sensory defects.
Avulsion: a tearing.

Callus: bony material between ends of a fractured bone when healing.
Cicatrix: scar.
Colles' fracture: fracture of wrist across the lower end of the radius.
Comminuted: bone fractured into several pieces.
Crepitus: grating of bone against bone or roughened cartilage.
Dorsiflexion: backward movement.
Embolism: blockage of small blood vessels.
Excise: to cut surgically.
Extension: straightening of a joint.
Fibrosis: thickening of tissue.
Flexion: bending of a joint.
Gluteal: of the buttock.
Ilium: hip bone.
Labial: of the lips.
Lesion: change in functions or texture of organs.
Lumbar: of the loins.
Manipulation: movement of a joint to reduce stiffness.
Node: small knot of tissue.
Odema: swelling due to build-up of fluid.
Parietal: referable to the inner walls of a body cavity.
Plantar: of sole of foot.
Pleural cavity: space between lungs and inner chest wall.
Pulmonary: of the lung.
Reduction: bringing back to normal position.
Sacrum: five fused vertebrae at base of spine.
Spondylosis: arthritis of the spine.
Thorax: of the chest.
Ulna: inner bone of the forearm.
Ureter: tubes taking urine from the pelvis to the bladder.

Check that the doctor has not discussed the cause of the accident, that there is no substantial disagreement between the doctor's and the plaintiff's account of the plaintiff's present condition, and for any suggestion by the doctor that the plaintiff is exaggerating the symptoms. Contact the doctor if there are such disagreements, or points in the report that are not clear (although you cannot draft the report for the expert). If still dissatisfied, obtain another report provided the client (and, where appropriate, the Legal Aid Board) approve.

The defendant's advisers will almost certainly want a report from their own doctor. Although they cannot insist on this, they can seek a stay of the action until the plaintiff undergoes a medical examination, unless the plaintiff's objection is a reasonable objection to being examined by a particular doctor, eg on the ground of a real risk of bias against the plaintiff. However, the plaintiff can insist on the following conditions:

- The plaintiff's expenses and any loss of earnings are paid.
- No one apart from the defendant's doctor is present.
- If the plaintiff is a minor, his or her parent can also be present.
- The doctor will not discuss the causes of the accident.

Note that the plaintiff *cannot* insist on seeing the defendant's report since this is privileged unless the defendant decides to use it at the trial, in which case it will be disclosed mutually with the plaintiff's (see Chapters 7 and 8).

4.4.3 Instructing engineers It is essential to instruct an expert in the appropriate field (eg mechanical or mining engineering) and who has experience of preparing reports for litigation. The Legal Practice Directorate of he Law Society or the area office of the Legal Aid Board may be able to suggest possible experts.

Also give the engineer as much information about the case as possible, including the client's and any witnesses' statements, the pleadings, if drafted, and plans and photographs of the accident site. Arrange an inspection of the site, and the defendant's undertaking that the relevant features such as the machine allegedly involved should not be altered in the meantime (see 4.3.1). Ensure that the expert is made clear as to the issues on which advice is required. Check the report when received and ensure that the client understands its implications.

4.5 Negotiations

4.5.1 'Without prejudice' correspondence Most of these claims, if successful, will ultimately be paid by insurers and will be handled initially by insurance companies' claims departments. It is their usual practice to conduct correspondence, often right up to settlement of the case, on the basis of a denial of liability and under the heading 'without prejudice'. The effect is to rely on the privilege from production of the letters in the proceedings without the writer's consent, except to prove the making and terms of any settlement reached (*Rush & Tompkins* v *Greater London Council* [1987] 2 WLR 533, CA). The privilege is attracted by any letter or other communication intended to make concessions or otherwise attempt to reach a settlement of a claim, although it is safer to use the words 'without prejudice' expressly.

4.5.2 Tactics   Advisers in personal injury cases should have two related aims. Firstly, they should each aim to discover as much as possible about their opponent's case while disclosing as little as possible of their own case. Secondly, they should try to keep up the pressure on their opponent. Accordingly, it is unwise to disclose too much detail in a letter before action or in early defence correspondence alleging contributory negligence. It is more effective for the plaintiff to serve the writ or summons quickly rather than to engage in protracted correspondence.

Once the action is under way, the defendant can put pressure back on the plaintiff by making a carefully calculated 'without prejudice' offer or payment into court (see 6.1) or by serving a Request for Further and Better Particulars. Both parties should seek to ensure that the case proceeds swiftly. It is not necessarily in the interests of defendants to protract matters (despite the opinion of some insurers to the contrary) since the level of damages constantly increases.

4.5.3 The 'without prejudice' discussion   Insurers or their solicitors will frequently seek to dispose of cases by means of such a discussion at the plaintiff's offices. It is important that both sides prepare thoroughly for such a meeting, checking the relevant law, the various heads of damage claimed and the current level of interest that would be awarded and of costs incurred. Insurers' claims representatives are likely to be well informed as to the going figure for the type of injuries in question, but there is likely to be scope for argument over the amount of contributory negligence, if any, and of the more speculative heads of damage. The plaintiff's lawyer should allow the defendant's lawyer to make the first offer. This is unlikely to be the last one, and it may be increased slightly if the plaintiff's adviser indicates that he or she cannot advise the client to accept it.

Once a definite offer has been made, the plaintiff's adviser should seek the client's instructions on it, explaining in particular the impact, if any, of the legal aid charge in respect of any costs not recovered from the defendant. Counsel's advice on the reasonableness of the settlement should be taken in cases of substance. The solicitor's oral advice should be confirmed in writing. If the client rejects the offer against the lawyers' advice in a legal aid case the Legal Aid Board should be informed and the certificate may be discharged (see 3.5.3).

For the procedural steps needed to terminate an action after settlement see Chapter 9.

4.6 Instructing counsel

4.6.1 When to use counsel Counsel are frequently instructed to advise on liability and quantum of damages at the outset of a personal injury action which is likely to proceed in the High Court (see 4.7). Such advice is usually in writing, a conference being reserved until a trial is in prospect. However, in difficult cases where the success of the party's case may depend, for example, on the party's credibility as a witness, it is helpful to have a conference and, perhaps, advice on evidence, at an earlier stage. Counsel will therefore be aware of the case when asked to draft the pleadings, and the client will be more confident that the case is being handled by someone who is familiar with it and whom he or she has met before the trial.

An added advantage for the solicitor is that if the case goes wrong through the action of counsel, the solicitor should be immune from liability in negligence, provided competent counsel was instructed and competently briefed (*In Re A (a minor)* (1988) **NLJ** 18 March, CA). While many generalist common law counsel will be able to handle ordinary road accident cases, you should take care to instruct more specialist counsel in complex factory or medical negligence cases.

4.6.2 How to instruct counsel Instructions should enclose all the relevant documents including the statements of the client and any witnesses, the police or Health and Safety Executive's and engineer's reports, the medical report(s), a calculation of special damage, any legal aid certificate and relevant correspondence with the other side. Instructions should not merely be a back sheet enclosing all the papers but be self-contained and self-explanatory, outlining the facts and the available evidence and specifying what counsel is being asked to do. This will minimise the difficulties if another counsel has to take over the case at a later date.

If the client is legally aided, then counsel will be paid direct by the Legal Aid Board. In other cases fees are on an agreed scale: see Chapter 10.3.

Once received, counsel's advice should be discussed with the client and its implications explained.

4.7 The decision to sue

4.7.1 To sue or not to sue? The decision must obviously be the client's, but should be made with the benefit of the solicitor's and, where necessary, counsel's advice, both oral and written. In particular, the risks of costs must be considered in both private and legally aided cases since legal aid contributions are now payable for the duration of a case. On the other hand, it may be essential to start proceedings because the limitation period is about to expire, or it may be desirable to do so to put pressure on the defendant to settle.

4.7.2   Where to sue   Whereas the maximum county court jurisdiction in tort is £5000, it was common until recently for actions expected to produce damages of at least £3000 to be taken in the High Court, this being the minimum figure at which High Court costs will be awarded (County Courts Act 1984, ss 19–20). The main reasons were probably the feeling that county court judges would be rather less generous in fixing the level of damages and that this would affect the attitude of insurers considering settlement of claims. Further, at present the High Court allows the parties more control over the conduct of the proceedings.

However, the High Court is also exerting more control over the progress of cases. Circuit judges are becoming more experienced at awarding larger amounts of damages as the High Court is increasingly using its powers to transfer cases to the county court if they think they are suitable for trial there, even though the amount in dispute would normally be outside the county court's jurisdiction (County Courts Act 1984, ss 41 and 42). Accordingly, it may be advisable to take proceedings for a claim exceeding £3000 but clearly below £5000 (ignoring contributory negligence and interest) in the county court. The rules as to which court office should be used are dealt with in Chapter 5.

4.8   Common problems and their solutions

Problem	*Solution*
Potential witnesses refuse to give statement.	Visit witnesses at home; point out that damages will be paid by insurers; threaten to subpoena them to give evidence at trial.
Insurers refuse to deal with claim because insured has not reported accident to them as required by the policy.	Point out that such policy conditions do not affect the insurers' duty to pay any judgment against their insured under Road Traffic Act 1972, s 149.
Facilities for inspecting	Threaten/apply for orders

factory accident site refused
or hospital refuses to
disclose treatment records in
medical negligence case.

Plaintiff's medical report
suggests plaintiff is
malingering.

Defendants will not increase
their first offer.

for pre-action inspection or
discovery of documents.

Suggest that the doctor
reconsiders in the light of
plaintiff's comments; or that
doctor put views in a
(privileged) covering letter;
or obtain another report.

Write stating that
proceedings will be started
unless the offer is increased
and asking for the details of
the solicitors who are to
accept service on the
defendants' behalf.

CHAPTER 5

STARTING PROCEEDINGS AND DRAFTING PLEADINGS

This chapter deals with the basic mechanics of starting court proceedings in personal injury cases and the basic principles of drafting the necessary pleadings. For more detail see O'Hare and Hill, *Civil Litigation*; and Pritchard, *Personal Injury Litigation*. An overview of the typical stages of High Court and county court personal injury actions is given by the diagrams on pages 48–49:

5.1 Issuing and serving the writ or summons.

These are the documents starting the action and telling the defendant of the claim.

5.1.1 High Court Take or send to the Central Office (for address, see Chapter 10) or any district registry, the following (RSC Ord 6):

- The writ (use Oyez Form 1 (unliquidated demand, PR or DR). The writ should contain a general indorsement stating the date and place of the accident, the fact it was caused by the defendant's negligence and/or breach of duty and caused the plaintiff loss and that the plaintiff claims damages. It should also claim interest on damages under Supreme Court Act 1981, s 35A. Only causes of action covered by the indorsement can be pleaded in the statement of claim, so if in doubt ask counsel to draft the indorsement of claim when drafting the statement of claim.

  If issuing the writ in the district registry for the area where the accident happened, indorsing the writ to that effect prevents the defendant seeking a transfer of the proceedings to another High Court office.

  At least three copies of the writ are needed, one signed by the plaintiff's solicitor for the court, one for the plaintiff (stamped 'original writ') and the others for service on the defendant(s).
- Court fee: 10.1.1.
- Next friend documentation if the plaintiff is a minor or mental patient. So long as they are under this disability such people can

Diagram A: Steps taken in typical QBD personal injury action

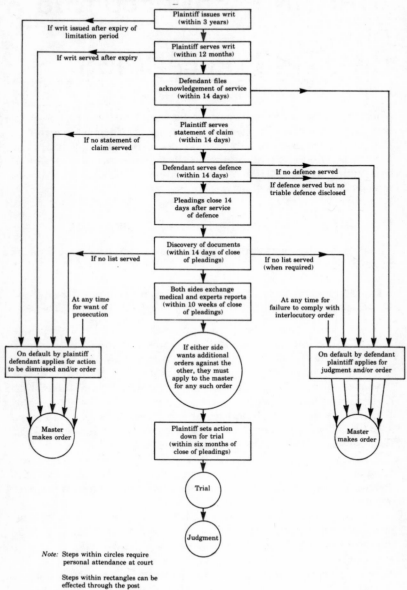

Note: Steps within circles require personal attendance at court

Steps within rectangles can be effected through the post

Diagram B: Steps taken in typical county court personal injury action

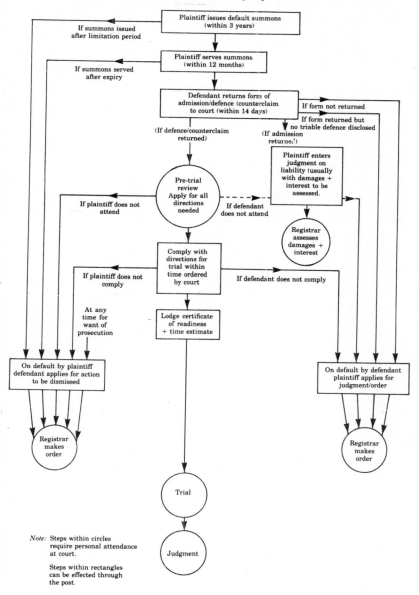

Plaintiff issues default summons
(within 3 years)

If summons issued after limitation period

Plaintiff serves summons
(within 12 months)

If summons served after expiry

Defendant returns form of admission/defence (counterclaim to court (within 14 days)

If form not returned

If form returned but no triable defence disclosed

(If defence/counterclaim returned)

(If admission returned)

Plaintiff enters judgment on liability (usually with damages + interest to be assessed.

Pre-trial review
Apply for all directions needed

If plaintiff does not attend

If defendant does not attend

Registrar assesses damages + interest

Comply with directions for trial within time ordered by court

If plaintiff does not comply

If defendant does not comply

At any time for want of prosecution

Lodge certificate of readiness + time estimate

On default by plaintiff defendant applies for action to be dismissed

On default by defendant plaintiff applies for judgment/order

Registrar makes order

Registrar makes order

Trial

Judgment

Note: Steps within circles require personal attendance at court.

Steps within rectangles can be effected through the post.

49

sue only through a next friend, who in the High Court must be represented by a solicitor. There must be filed the next friend's consent to act and solicitor's certificate of no conflict of interest. The name of the next friend is added to the title of the action thus:

AB (a minor) by CD his mother and next friend   Plaintiff
and
EF   Defendant

- Legal aid certificate if any, and notice of issue.

The court assigns an action number to the case and seals and returns the unsigned copies.

If the defendant in a road accident case is insured, preserve the plaintiff's rights to enforce the judgment against the defendant's insurers under Road Traffic Act 1972, s 149 by informing the insurers of the issue of proceedings within seven days (see 1.2.2). However, if the defendant is not insured, preserve the plaintiff's rights to enforce any judgment against the Motor Insurers' Bureau by informing them of the issue of proceedings within seven days.

If the writ contains errors, or changes to the parties or causes of action are desired, amend the writ before service since leave of the court is not needed at this stage (RSC Ord 6).

The plaintiff has twelve months in which to serve the writ, but the writ may be renewed for good cause, eg if the defendant has gone abroad, but not necessarily merely because the defendant has continued negotiations (RSC Ord 6, r 8). If the writ remains unserved for no good reason the defendant can require the plaintiff to serve it within a prescribed period or discontinue the action (RSC Ord 12A).

The following documents must be served on the defendant (RSC Ord 10, r 1(6)):

- Sealed copy writ.
- Statement of claim (if desired). It may be preferable to defer service of the statement of claim if further inquiries are needed or where the service of the writ alone may spur on a settlement.
- Acknowledgement of service form. Use Oyez Form 22.
- Notice of issue of legal aid certificate where appropriate.

The writ can be served by the following methods (see Radevsky, *Service of Documents*):

- On individual defendants. By personal service (immediate) or by ordinary first class post (or by placing the writ in the defendant's letter box) when it is effected seven days after posting including weekends and bank holidays (RSC Ord 10, r 1 (1–3)). However, postal service may not bring the writ to the defendant's notice so it is dangerous if the defendant is evasive or a limitation period is near expiry.

- On limited companies. Serve by posting or leaving the writ at the company's registered office. Service is effected on the second working day after posting (first class post) or the fourth working day after posting (second class post) (Companies Act 1985, s 725).
- On a partnership. If (as is usual) the firm is sued in the firm's name, serve the writ personally on any partner or serve any person having control of the business at the firm's principal place of business (RSC Ord 81, r 3).
- On the defendant's solicitors. Ask the defendant's insurers to nominate solicitors to accept service. Then write to them with the copy writ and acknowledgement of service asking them to accept service. The original writ does not require indorsement to this effect (RSC Ord 10, r 1 (5)).
- By substituted service if other methods fail, apply to the court for a direction as to the method to be used, eg leaving the writ at the defendant's last known address and also giving details in a local newspaper for that area (RSC Ord 65, r 4).

5.1.2 County court You will need to issue a default summons. Take or send to the court for the district where the accident happened or where the defendant lives or carries on business the following (CCR Ord 3):

- Request for the issue of a default summons: this is prescribed form N201. State the claim is for damages (limited to £5000) for personal injuries and loss, with costs to be taxed.
- Particulars of claim. General principles of pleading are discussed later in this chapter but note that interest on damages should be claimed citing County Courts Act 1984, s 69. It is not normally appropriate in personal injury cases to indorse the particulars on the request for the summons. One copy of the particulars is needed for the court and one for each defendant.
- Court fee (see 10.2).
- Where the plaintiff is a child or mental patient, the next friend's combined form of consent to act and undertaking to be responsible should the plaintiff not pay any costs awarded against him. This must be signed in front of a solicitor or court officer (CCR Ord 10, r 2). No separate certificate of no conflict of interest is needed.
- Legal aid certificate and notice of issue for each defendant, if appropriate.

- Default summons in prescribed form N2 (unliquidated claim) if desired, eg to save time if the court office is very busy.

The court office assigns a case number and sends the plaintiff a plaint note, and if the solicitor is effecting service, the summons.

The following documents must be served on the defendant:

- Sealed summons.
- Particulars of claim.
- Form of admission, defence and counterclaim (supplied by the court).
- Notice of issue of legal aid certificate if appropriate.

Service is effected as in the High Court but note:

- The court fee includes postal service by the court. However, if this does not reach the defendant, the judgment can be set aside.
- The court bailiff will attempt personal service if postal service has failed on payment of a further fee (see 10.2) but service by inquiry agent may be more effective.

5.2 Acknowledging service in the High Court (RSC Ord 12)

5.2.1 Time The defendant must return the acknowledgement of service form to the court office issuing it within fourteen days of service including the day of service, unless an extension of time has been agreed between the parties or ordered by the court. If returned by post, the date of acknowledgement is the date of receipt by the court which stamps it on the acknowledgement and sends a copy to the plaintiff.

If the form is not returned in time the plaintiff can seek judgment in default under Ord 13. This will be interlocutory judgment on liability, with damages and interest to be assessed later and costs to be taxed (see 9.3.1).

5.2.2 Who may complete the acknowledgment? The following may complete the form:

- An individual defendant or his solicitor.
- A solicitor or other authorised person on behalf of a limited company.
- A partner in the defendant firm.
- A solicitor for the guardian ad litem of a child or mental patient (thus the guardian's consent to act and solicitor's certificate of no conflict of interest must also be filed).

5.2.3 Possible indorsements   The following may be indorsed on the form:

• Notice of intention to defend although if the defendant states that he or she will not be defending, the plaintiff can seek judgment in default under RSC Ord 13 as above.
• Application for transfer to another district registry or the Central Office. This may be more convenient for the defendant but cannot be done if the plaintiff has stated on the writ that the cause of action arose in the district of that district registry.
• Defendant's address for service.

5.3   Statement or particulars of claim

5.3.1 Time for service   The High Court statement of claim must, in the absence of the agreement of the parties or order of the court, be served with the writ or within fourteen days of the defendant giving notice of intention to defend (RSC Ord 18, r 1). However, it is common to grant a reasonable extension of time for serving this and other pleadings; if you do not, your opponent can take out a summons for more time (RSC Ord 3, r 5).

The particulars of claim in the county court must be served with the summons; time for serving later pleadings may be extended as in the High Court.

5.3.2 Use of counsel   In the High Court it is normally best to instruct counsel to draft the statement of claim (and, in complex cases, the indorsement of claim on the writ) as counsel would have to appear at any trial. For guidance on preparing the instructions, see 4.6.

5.3.3 Principles of pleading (RSC Ord 18)   These are the same for both the High Court and the county court. Make concise allegations of relevant fact, not matters of fine detail or evidence to be used to prove the allegations. Generally, the plaintiff cannot plead matters of law, nor anticipate possible defence arguments. But the parties must give enough detail of their allegations that the opponent knows the case to be met; otherwise, the opponent can serve a request, and if this is not complied with, obtain an order, for further and better particulars of the pleading.

The general framework of the statement or particulars of claim is as follows (see Chapter 11 for a precedent):

• Outline of the history of the incident.

- Allegation that incident occurred due to defendant's negligence or breach of statutory duty.
- Particulars of negligence etc.
- Allegation that such negligence caused plaintiff loss.
- Particulars of plaintiff's losses, firstly particulars of injuries (from the medical report) then particulars of special damage, including any continuing losses.
- Claim for interest on damages under Supreme Court Act 1981, s 35A or County Courts Act 1984, s 69 including any facts justifying a higher than usual interest rate.
- Prayer for damages, unquantified save that they must be limited to £5000 maximum in county court cases, and interest.

It is important to note that the following must be specifically pleaded:

- (On the statement of claim) the date of issue of the writ.
- The plaintiff's date of birth and any unusual current or future losses such as effect on leisure interests or career prospects.
- Any relevant convictions of the defendant, stating the date, court convicting, nature of the conviction and its relevance to the proceedings (Civil Evidence Act 1968, s 11).
- Any claim for provisional damages.

5.4 Defences and counterclaims

5.4.1 Time for service In the High Court these must be served within fourteen days from service of the statement of claim, if not served with the writ; fourteen days after the time for acknowledging service of the writ if the statement of claim is served with the writ (RSC Ord 18, r 2).

In the county court: the form of admission or defence or counterclaim (prescribed form N9 or a document in the ordinary (High Court) format) must be returned to the court within fourteen days of service of the summons, excluding the day of service (CCR Ord 9, rr 1, 2). If the ordinary form is used, a copy must be supplied for each plaintiff.

In each case failure to comply enables the plaintiff to obtain judgment in default of defence (RSC Ord 19; CCR Ord 9) on liability, with damages and interest to be assessed and costs to be taxed (see 9.3.1).

5.4.2 Use of counsel See 5.3.2.

5.4.3 Drafting the defence and/or counterclaim The defendant must deny every allegation by the plaintiff which can be disputed or he or she will be deemed to admit them. A general denial of the allegations as if they set out and individually denied is not sufficient by itself. Nor is the bare denial or 'holding' defence which does not state any grounds. However, it is permissible to take points of law such as limitation or that the statement of claim discloses no cause of action.

The usual format is as follows (see Chapter 11 for a precedent):

- Admit the accident and any other matters that cannot be disputed.
- Deny that the accident was the result of any negligence or breach of duty by the defendant.
- Allege the accident was the result of negligence by the plaintiff (contributory negligence).
- Give particulars of any negligence by the plaintiff.
- If appropriate allege the accident was the result of negligence by some other person. If that person is not yet a party, then a third party notice should be issued and served before serving the defence (RSC Ord 16; CCR Ord 12). The third party notice should be in prescribed forms 20 or 21 (High Court) or N15 (county court). See Chapter 6.
- Make no admissions regarding the allegations of loss and damage.
- Any counterclaim should be in the same document, immediately after the defence. If it relates to the same incident it is usually sufficient to refer back to the allegations in the defence. Otherwise the negligence or other wrong by the plaintiff must be alleged and particulars given.
- The defendant must allege that the plaintiff's wrongful act has caused loss and give particulars of such loss.
- The defendant claims interest on damages under Supreme Court Act 1981, s 35A or County Courts Act 1984, s 69.
- Prayer for damages and interest under the relevant statutory provision.

The following must be specifically pleaded:

- Limitation.
- Contributory negligence.
- Denials that the defendant has been convicted as alleged or allegations that the conviction is irrelevant or erroneous.

The detail required in most defences and counterclaims makes the county court supplied form of defence, admission or counterclaim inappropriate. The High Court format should be adopted and the original filed at court with a copy for each plaintiff.

5.5 Reply and/or defence to counterclaim

5.5.1 Are they necessary? It is never mandatory to serve a reply since the plaintiff is deemed to deny allegations in the defence (RSC Ord 18, r 14). However, a reply is desirable to deal with points not covered in the statement of claim, eg contributory negligence. If the plaintiff wishes to change the basic story this should be done by amending the statement of claim.

It is essential, however, in the High Court to serve a defence to counterclaim since otherwise the defendant can enter judgment in default under Ord 19. The position is in effect the same in the county court since if no defence to counterclaim is filed the defendant will probably get judgment on the counterclaim at the pre-trial review. See 9.3.1.

5.5.2 Time limits for serving a reply etc In the High Court, the time limit is fourteen days from service of the defence or counterclaim (RSC Ord 18, r 3).

In the county court, there are no specific rules. If the plaintiff wants to serve a reply a direction should be sought at the pre-trial review.

5.5.3 Notice to insurers If the plaintiff is insured, the insurers should be notified of any counterclaim or they might be able to repudiate liability to meet it. They should also be asked if they wish the plaintiff's solicitors to act for them on the counterclaim.

5.5.4 Closure of pleadings or pre-trial review In the High Court, pleadings close fourteen days after service of the reply or defence to counterclaim; otherwise fourteen days after service of the defence (RSC Ord 18, r 20). This date should be noted since the fourteen day time limit for discovery runs from this date.

In the county court once a defence is served, judgment in default is impossible and a pre-trial review date will be fixed by the court.

CHAPTER 6

PAYMENTS INTO COURT, THIRD PARTY PROCEEDINGS, INTERIM PAYMENTS

This chapter will deal with two major defence tactics, payments into court and third party proceedings, and the important plaintiff's tactic of interim payments. For more detail see Pritchard, *Personal Injury Litigation* and O'Hare and Hill, *Civil Litigation*.

6.1 Payments into court (RSC Ord 22; CCR Ord 11)

6.1.1 The purpose of payments in It can be unfair to defendants to have actions hanging over them, which are not of their choosing and which may have little merit. To counter the powerful weapon of a writ or summons, the defendant may at any time after service of proceedings but before judgment without admitting liability pay money into court in satisfaction of the claim. If the plaintiff accepts it, he or she will be entitled to his costs. Providing the payment in is made at least twenty one days before the trial and if the plaintiff rejects it and fails to recover more at the trial the plaintiff will have to pay the defendant's costs incurred after the payment in, although the plaintiff's own costs up to that point can be recovered.

A carefully calculated payment in is therefore an important tactical defence weapon since the costs risk puts great pressure on the plaintiff to settle for rather less than might be received at a trial. The best defence tactic is probably to make the payment in early in the action, to maximise the risk of later costs, and to make one, or at the most two payments (to make more smacks of weakness). The payment must be sufficiently large as to put real doubt into the mind of the plaintiff's advisers that it is likely to be beaten at the trial, while offering a real saving to the defendant.

Note that the payment in is of value to the defence not only where the plaintiff is funding the action, but also where he is legally aided. This is because the defendant's solicitor will have to inform the Legal Aid Board if a payment in is made and if the plaintiff unreasonably refuses the payment the legal aid certificate will probably be discharged (see Chapter 3). Further, the post-payment in costs awarded to the defendant if the payment in is not beaten at the trial will be set off against the damages payable by the defendant. Much or all of the rest of the damages will be eaten up by the statutory charge in respect of the plaintiff's own legal costs.

Because of these risks, the plaintiff's solicitors must advise the client carefully both orally and in writing and in a substantial case obtain counsel's advice.

6.1.2 Procedure: High Court The procedure for making the payment in is as follows:

1 Plaintiff takes or sends to Court Funds Office, Royal Courts of Justice or district registry:

> request for lodgment (Oyez Form E33); cheque or bank draft payable to Accountant General of Supreme Court; copy writ; notice of payment in (Oyez Form B5) specifying in respect of which causes of action it is made, whether it takes account of any counterclaim or interim payment, and the amount of interest included.

2 Court stamps notice of payment in and returns it to defendant.
3 Defendant sends notice of payment in to plaintiff and other defendants.
4 Plaintiff sends written acknowledgment of receipt of notice within three days (to enable defendant to calculate time for acceptance).

For acceptance of payment in, the procedure is:

1 Plaintiff sends notice of acceptance (Oyez Form B82) to all defendants within twenty-one days of receipt of notice of payment in. (Issue summons if accepting late, if payment is not by all defendants, in fatal cases or if plaintiff a minor or mental patient.)
2 Plaintiff sends or takes to Court Funds Office or district registry:

> stamped notice of payment in;
> copy notice of acceptance;
> request for payment out (Oyez Form B80);
> two copies of payment schedule (Oyez Form B84).

3 Action stayed, cheque sent to plaintiff (to plaintiff's solicitor if legally aided).
4 Plaintiff can submit bill for taxation four days after payment out.

if costs not agreed, and sign judgment for them two days after taxation.

For non-acceptance of the payment in, the procedure is:

1 No notice to defendant needed.
2 Court puts payment on deposit for defendant after two days; no withdrawal without leave of court.
3 Payment in must not be mentioned in pleadings or at trial until judgment given.
4 After judgment court told of payment in with regard to liability for costs (see 3.2.4)

6.1.3 Procedure: county court When making the payment in, the procedure is as follows:

1 Defendant sends or takes to county court:
   cheque or draft payable to HMPG; letter asking that money be paid in in satisfaction of the claim (or use Oyez Form 1006).
2 Court sends receipt to defendant and notice of payment in to all parties.

For acceptance of payment in the procedure is:

1 Within twenty-one days of receiving notice of payment in plaintiff sends notice of acceptance (Oyez Form 1007) to all defendants and copy to court. (Notice of application needed if accepting late if payment is not by all defendants, if payment is in fatal cases or where plaintiff is a minor or mental patient.)
2 Plaintiff submits bill for taxation.
3 Proceedings stayed, court pays out money (to solicitor if plaintiff legally aided).

For non-acceptance of the payment in the position is as in the High Court.

6.1.4 Provisional damages The defendant may make a written offer of a stated amount on the basis that the plaintiff's condition will not deteriorate and offer to submit to an award of provisional damages in that sum. If this is refused, the offer will only be mentioned to the judge after the trial and the costs consequences will be the same as if it had been a payment into court (RSC Ord 37, r 9).

6.1.5 Split trials After the making of an order that liability be tried before quantum of damages (see 7.1.2) the defendant may make a written offer to any other party to accept liability up to a specified proportion (RSC Ord 33, r 4A). This will have the same effect as a payment into court if the defendant is held to be no more to blame than the proportion offered. This is therefore a good means for a defendant to redress the extra pressure he or she may be put under by a split trial; it may also be a way of forcing a co-defendant to join in a settlement.

6.2 Third party proceedings

6.2.1 Purpose of third party proceedings (RSC Ord 16; CCR Ord 12) A defendant (including a plaintiff who is defending a counterclaim) who wants to blame or otherwise make a claim or have a question decided against someone not yet a party to the proceedings could, of course, do so by starting fresh proceedings. However, this would be expensive, time consuming and there would be no guarantee that consistent results would be reached in the two sets of proceedings. Accordingly, it is better generally for such claims to be pursued by means of third party proceedings. These are, in theory, separate from the main action, so that if the accident is held to have been the fault of the third party, and not the defendant, the plaintiff will recover nothing from the defendant. The third party should have been joined as a second defendant (see 6.2.5).

6.2.2. Claims that can be raised The usual claims against third parties in personal injury actions are:
- Contribution or indemnity, ie partial or full reimbursement of whatever damages, if any, the defendant has to pay the plaintiff. An example would be a defendant driver's claim that a garage serviced his or her car negligently and should refund any damages paid to another road user injured in the resulting accident.
- Claim for relief similar to that claimed by the plaintiff. Such a claim can be made if it arises out of the same facts as the plaintiff's claim. An example would be a defendant's claim that a garage negligently serviced his or her car and should pay damages for the damage caused to the car in the resulting collision.

6.2.3 Procedure: High Court

1 Any time after defendant given notice of intention to defend. (No leave needed if issuing before Defence served.) (Obtain amendment to legal aid certificate.)
2 Defendant issues Third Party Notice in Oyez Form B1 giving nature and grounds of claim and remedy sought. (Not needed if

one defendant just seeks contribution from other defendant but notify of claim by letter).

3 Defendant serves third party notice on third party as if it were a writ, with copy of writ and pleadings and acknowledgment of service: and sends copy notice to plaintiff.

4 Third party acknowledges service within fourteen days. (In default third party deemed to admit claims and bound by any judgment.)

5 Defendant issues summons for third party directions in Oyez Form S33.

6 Defendant serves summons on all parties.

7 Hearing of summons: usual orders include:

third party pleadings;
discovery between third party and other parties;
leave for plaintiff to join third party as extra defendant;
directions for trial of third party issue (usually immediately after main trial) and for participation of third party in main trial.

6.2.4   Procedure: county court

1 No leave needed if issuing before date fixed for pre-trial review, ie if before or when serving defence. (Obtain amendment to legal aid certificate.)

2 Defendant files at court three copies of third party notice (Prescribed Form N15) and two sets of pleadings. (Plaintiff cannot now enter judgment in default or on admissions.)

3 Court endorses date for pre-trial review of third party action (normally immediately after pre-trial review in main action) and serves notice and copies of the summons and pleadings on the third party as if notice were a summons.

4 Third party serves a defence within fourteen days. (In default court may order service of defence or be debarred from defending.)

5 Pre-trial review (see 6.2.3 for usual orders).

6 At the trial: the third party can play such part as court allows. (If third party fails to attend, is bound by judgment in main action and deemed to admit claim against him/her even if filed a defence.)

6.2.5 Joining in a third party   It is essential for the plaintiff to sue the right person. If the defendant brings in a third party, X, and it seems possible that X will be found wholly to blame, the plaintiff must seriously consider joining X as a second defendant. If the plaintiff does not do so and then X is found wholly at fault, the plaintiff will fail against the defendant and have to pay costs and will then be put to the trouble and expense of suing X separately.

However, to join in extra parties the party wanting the joinder will either have to obtain the leave of the court (rarely given) or show the parties are closely connected to the incident in question: a common question of law or fact must arise and all the rights to relief must arise out of the same transaction or series of transactions (RSC Ord 15, r 4; CCR Ord 5, r 2). An example would be where a pedestrian claims against both the driver involved and also his garage which negligently serviced the car.

Even where such leave is not needed it will be necessary to obtain an amendment to any legal aid certificate and to obtain leave to amend the writ or summons and the statement or particulars of claim once served (RSC Ord 20, r 5; CCR Ord 7, r 17). Leave will generally be given on payment of the opponent's costs unless the limitation period has expired. Amendments are typed in red and the date and authority for the amendment indorsed. The amended documents must then be served on all parties, who can then serve amended pleadings in reply. See generally RSC Ord 20 and CCR Ord 15.

6.3 Interim payments

6.3.1 Purpose of and grounds for interim payments (RSC Ord 29; CCR Ord 13) These payments are payments on account of any damages which the defendant may be ordered to pay. They are designed to meet the complaint that plaintiffs with strong cases often have to wait long periods before receiving any compensation, eg because the plaintiff's medical position has not yet stabilised. Plaintiffs' solicitors should often consider applying for these since they can greatly reduce any financial hardship the plaintiff may be suffering (though they are not limited to such cases). They may also be a means of financing the action in the absence of legal aid (see Chapter 3).

While defendants may wish to oppose such applications, there is the advantage to defendants that the plaintiff will have to disclose certain information, particularly the medical evidence, before this would otherwise have to be done.

To obtain a payment, the plaintiff has to show one of the following:

- The defendant has admitted liability. This will be rare.
- The plaintiff has obtained judgment on liability with damages to be assessed. Split trials are fairly rare although they are an alternative to the provisional damages procedure where the medical condition may worsen in the medium term. See 7.1.2.
- If the action proceeds to trial the plaintiff is likely to obtain substantial damages. This will be the ground most commonly used. Note that this may be the case even though the plaintiff may be held contributorily negligent if the injuries are serious enough.

However, the Court of Appeal has recently stressed that the plaintiff must show that recovery is likely and not merely possible (*Gibbons* v *Wall* (1988) *The Times*, 24 February.

6.3.2 Defences The court cannot order an interim payment in a personal injury action unless the defendant is either:

- Insured in respect of the plaintiff's claim. ✗
- A public authority; or
- A person whose resources are such as to enable him to make an interim payment.

In particular, an interim payment will not be awarded against the Motor Insurers' Bureau (*Powney* v *Coxage* (1988) *The Times*, 8 March, although the MIB may volunteer a payment.

6.3.3 Procedure: High Court
1 Plaintiff asks defendant for voluntary payment.
2 If no payment volunteered, plaintiff issues summons for order for interim payment with affidavit in support which is stamped but not filed at court. (Affidavit details special damage to date, the medical evidence and the plaintiff's reasons for thinking he will recover substantial damages: see Chapter 11 for precedent.)
3 Plaintiff serves copy summons and affidavit on defendant at least ten clear days before hearing.
4 Summons heard: if payment ordered often covers special damage to date (though no reason why cannot be more). Plaintiff should seek interest on payment if trial still far off. (Once payment ordered, plaintiff cannot discontinue without leave.)
   Master or district registrar can give directions for conduct of rest of case.
5 Defendant sends payment direct to plaintiff (exempt from legal aid statutory charge and will not cause re-assessment of eligibility for legal aid but, if £6000 or more, will disqualify from obtaining social security benefits). Payment not pleaded or mentioned at trial until after judgment.
6 At trial if plaintiff awarded less than interim payment repayment may be ordered. If recovers more than interim payment, judgment given for unpaid balance, payment being set first against special damages, then generals. (Any payment into court should now be stated to take account of interim payment.)

6.3.4 Procedure: county court This is essentially the same as in the High Court with the following minor differences:

- The sum claimed must exceed £500. This covers virtually all personal injury claims.
- Application is by notice of application and affidavit, served at least seven days before the hearing.
- The hearing may be treated as a pre-trial review.

6.4 Common problems and their solutions

Problem	*Solution*
Defendant makes payment into court.	Plaintiff's solicitor reviews liability, quantum and evidence, obtains counsel's opinion on payment if case substantial, and advises client orally and in writing.
Payment into court does not include interest.	Although defendant not bound to include interest, if none included plaintiff can threaten/continue action to recover the interest.
Can the payment in be passed on to the client if accepted?	Yes, except where the plaintiff is legally aided (Legal Aid Board leave needed) or a minor or mental patient (payment needs court's consent and money stays in court: see Chapter 9.2).
Defendant issues third party notice.	Plaintiff should usually join in third party as an additional defendant if there is a cause of action against the third party.
Plaintiff seeks large interim payment.	Defendant should review liability (particularly contributory negligence) and quantum and oppose application; or offer payment covering special damages to date less deduction for contributory negligence; and/or make a payment into court.

CHAPTER 7

DIRECTIONS AND DISCOVERY

The period after close of pleadings is an important one. A party who uses effectively the range of interlocutory applications (those made after the action starts but before trial) can score a significant advantage over the lazier party. Both sides should try to keep the momentum up with the aim of pressurising the other and, perhaps, securing a favourable settlement.

Directions generally will be dealt with first. These enable the court to consider the preparations for the trial and make any orders that may be needed. We will then consider the important topic of discovery, ie disclosure of documents. For the possibility of obtaining discovery before the action starts see 3.2.

For more detail see O'Hare and Hill, *Civil Litigation*, Pritchard, *Personal Injury Litigation*, and Style and Hollander, *Documentary Evidence*.

7.1   Directions in the High Court (RSC Ord 25)

7.1.1   Automatic directions These apply in personal injury actions, ie actions in which there is a claim for personal injuries (including disease) or death, but not medical negligence (RSC Ord 1, r 4).

After close of pleadings (see 5.5.4) the following directions take effect automatically, without any application to the court being needed (RSC Ord 25, r 8):

- Discovery of documents must take place within fourteen days of close of pleadings and inspection within seven days afterwards. However, where liability is admitted or the action arises out of a road accident, discovery is limited to disclosure by the plaintiff of any documents relating to special damage, eg details of social security benefits received but not details of his injuries. The defendant does not have to give discovery at all under this rule. (A road accident means an accident on land due to a collision or apprehended collision involving a vehicle.)
- Where a party wants to use expert evidence at the trial he must,

within ten weeks, disclose the substance of that evidence in the form of a report to the other parties and it should be agreed if possible. Notice that this would not cover additional comments made by the expert to the instructing solicitors in a covering letter, nor reports which are not to be used at the trial. These are privileged and can stay at the back of the file.

Disclosure of the reports must be on a mutual basis, ie medical for medical, non-medical for non-medical, and simultaneous (although, in practice, the defendant's solicitors may try to delay sending their report until they receive the plaintiff's, in order to see if it is less helpful to the plaintiff than their own).

If the reports cannot be agreed, the parties can call the authors, up to a maximum of two medical and one non-medical expert.

- Photographs, sketch plans and any police report are receivable in evidence without calling the people who made them, and should be agreed if possible.
- The place of trial will be the trial centre for the place where the action is proceeding, ie the Royal Courts of Justice if the action is in the Principal Registry, the designated court centre in district registry cases, unless the parties agree otherwise in writing.
- The mode of trial will be by a judge alone, without a jury, as a category B case (categories A–C depending on difficulty).
- Setting down for trial must be done within six months (see 9.1) and the court notified on setting down of the estimated length of the trial.

7.1.2 Other directions: the summons for directions The automatic directions will not be available in medical negligence cases. Even if available, they will sometimes not be complied with; more often, the imaginative solicitor will want different or additional orders, for example:

- Discovery by a defendant in a road accident case. See *Rickett* v *Roadcraft (Crane and Plant Hire)* [1987] 6 CL 296.
- Directions regarding expert evidence. Where the automatic directions do not apply, expert evidence cannot be adduced at the trial without the leave of the court or all parties' agreement. The court's leave will now in all cases (including medical negligence) be subject to prior disclosure of the report, unless there is sufficient reason for not doing so (RSC Ord 38, rr 37, 38 as amended). However, there would be sufficient reason for non-disclosure if a medical report discussed how the injuries occurred or the genuineness of the symptoms, or a non-medical report is based on a disputed version of the facts or on facts not ascertainable from the expert's

own observations or expertise. The parties might also want leave to call more than the usual number of experts, eg more specialist doctors where the injuries are complex and serious.

- If a more detailed plan than a sketch plan is needed then this must be made available for inspection by the other parties at least ten days before the trial (RSC Ord 38, r 5).
- The deciding factors for the place of trial should be where is most convenient for the parties and their witnesses.
- Ensure that the listing category for the mode of trial is correct. The plaintiff might want to seek a split trial; the defendant may wish to consider an application for transfer of the action to the county court: see 8.6.2.
- Other orders may include leave to amend pleadings; orders for further and better particulars of pleadings; and preservation and inspection of property (important in many factory cases, if not already obtained on pre-action inspection of property—see Chapter 4). Both parties should seek now any orders they may want for the rest of the case, since an application later may be penalised in costs. The summons for directions also has the potential value of forcing the parties to take stock of their cases. Particularly if the solicitors meet (perhaps for the first time) there is the chance that a settlement offer may be forthcoming. Indeed, the court has to secure all reasonable agreements and admissions, and record refusals to make such admissions. This may be useful later on the question of costs.

7.1.3   Summons for directions: procedure if orders not agreed

1 Within one month of close of pleadings the plaintiff takes/sends to Action Department, Royal Courts of Justice or district registry: a completed form of summons for directions in Oyez Form S30. Strike out the numbers of items not wanted and complete those items that are wanted; fee (see Chapter 11).

2 Court inserts hearing date and returns summons to plaintiff.

3 Plaintiff serves copy summons on other parties at least fourteen clear days before the hearing date.

4 Defendant gives notice using Form PF52 of any orders he wants that are different from those sought by the plaintiff, at least seven days before the hearing.

5 Hearing of the summons: both parties must attend. Plaintiff hands master or district registrar the summons and a set of pleadings. Master makes orders.

6 Plaintiff takes/sends to Action Department or district registry top copy summons initialled and dated by master and proposed order

in Oyez Form H2/H2A (DR) drafted by the plaintiff and copy.
7 Court initials and seals order and copy, files copy and returns original to plaintiff.
8 Plaintiff serves copy order on each party.

7.1.4 Summons for directions: orders agreed: consent summonses

1 Plaintiff prepares draft order in Form H2/H2A.
2 Plaintiff sends draft order to defendant's solicitors asking them to indorse their consent.
3 Plaintiff attends before master/or district registrar who approves draft order.
4 Plaintiff takes/sends to court draft order and copy (no fee).
5 Court initials and seals original order, files copy and returns original to plaintiff.
6 Plaintiff serves copy order on other parties.

7.2 Directions in the county court (CCR Ord 17)

7.2.1 Orders that may be sought There are no automatic directions in the county court: a pre-trial review must be held when directions can be sought. The court will have informed the parties of the date fixed for the pre-trial review as soon as the defence is filed.

The orders commonly made at the pre-trial review are usually similar to those made in the High Court. However, because the pre-trial review is held earlier than the summons for directions it may well be desirable to seek more extensive orders. Examples are:

- Orders for further pleadings, eg a reply or defence to counterclaim.
- Orders for further and better particulars of pleadings.
- Discovery and inspection of documents (this is not automatic in the county court: see 7.4).
- Directions as to evidence, particularly expert evidence.
- Directions for trial (usually the court orders that the trial date will be fixed on both parties certifying they are ready and filing a time estimate).

Note that the court can give judgment for the plaintiff if the defendant makes an admission, or fails to attend the pre-trial review or is in default of an 'unless' order imposed for failure to take some interlocutory step such as filing a pleading within a stated time. Such judgment will be interlocutory with damages to be assessed.

7.2.2 Procedure It is good practice to notify the court and the other side of the orders you are going to seek, a letter to this effect being sufficient. No court fee is payable. The court considers the orders sought. These are so standard in most cases that many courts have their own standard form of directions. Further, the inconvenience of having to attend what is often a formality can often be avoided by the plaintiff lodging a draft order indorsed with the defendant's consent. The court will then seal it and serve it on the parties.

7.3   Discovery in the High Court (RSC Ord 24)

7.3.1   Purpose of discovery   Discovery is the disclosure by one party to the other of the existence of relevant documents that are or have been in his or her possession or power and the provision of facilities for inspection of those documents, other than those for which the party giving discovery claims privilege. It should enable the parties to test the strength of their cases and so perhaps encourage a settlement and in any event it is difficult to deal with documentary evidence for the first time at the trial.

Accordingly, it is an important topic, but one that is often taken insufficiently seriously in personal injury claims because solicitors often feel that it is unlikely that there will be any relevant documents.

Remember that it is the solicitors' duty to obtain from the client and preserve any relevant documents, however embarrassing they may be to the client's case. The solicitor cannot be a party to such documents disappearing! Further, disclosed documents may only be used for the purpose of the current proceedings, unless they have been read out in open court (RSC Ord 24, r 14A), or unless the party obtaining discovery applies to be released from this obligation.

7.3.2   Documents to look out for

- Accident book kept by employer under the Factories Act 1961— look for entries regarding the current and previous similar accidents.
- Employer's complaints book.
- Minutes of any safety committee under the Health and Safety at Work Act 1974.
- Statements made to the employer or hospital after the accident if not made mainly with regard to future litigation.
- Maintenance records of machine or vehicles involved in the accident.
- DHSS Form B176 completed by the employer if the employee

claims disablement benefit. The employer briefly describes how the accident happened.

- Form 2508 (notification of accident to Health and Safety Executive). This must be completed in respect of any accident causing death or major injury, ie generally one resulting in more than twenty-four hours' treatment in hospital.
- Employee's sick notes.
- Plaintiff's special damage documents. These will be needed in all cases, even road accidents where there may be no documents relevant to liability. These include eg letters from the employer regarding lost earnings and statutory sick pay and from the DHSS regarding other state benefits.

7.3.3 Procedure: automatic discovery This is provided in the rules, without the need for a court order, in all writ actions except in the following:

- In third party proceedings there is no discovery unless the court so orders (see 6.2.3).
- In cases where liability is admitted.
- In road accident cases there is no automatic discovery by the defendant and the plaintiff only needs to disclose documents relating to special damage.

Under RSC Ord 24, rr 2, 5 discovery must be made by the parties exchanging lists of documents in Oyez Form B9 within fourteen days of close of pleadings. Schedule 1, Pt 1 lists those documents in the party's possession he or she does not object to producing, eg the plaintiff's special damage documents. Part 2 lists those documents the party objects to producing on the ground of privilege. These will include 'without prejudice' correspondence between the parties, correspondence with the client and with witnesses about the case, including experts' reports and instructions to counsel and counsel's advice. Remember that for privilege to apply the dominant purpose of the document (*Waugh* v *British Railways Board* [1979] 2 All ER 1169) must have been the giving or receiving of advice or information in connection with actual or reasonably foreseeable proceedings (*Guiness Peat Properties* v *Fitzroy Robinson* [1987] 2 All ER 716, CA).

Schedule 2 lists those documents which the party no longer has, generally the originals of correspondence in the case.

The list must also state where and when the documents can be inspected. The opponent can require that the party giving discovery supply copies of the documents in Sched 1, Pt 1 on payment of copying charges (RSC Ord 24, r 11A).

7.3.4   Procedure: orders for discovery   Where the provisions for automatic discovery do not apply or are inadequate or the party concerned fails to comply with them, apply for general discovery by means of a list of all or a class of the opponent's documents (RSC Ord 24, r 3). The application is made by way of summons. If you do not trust the opponent to give full disclosure, ask the court to order the opponent to swear an affidavit verifying the completeness of the list (Oyez Form B8A). The court can also order the making of a further and better list if the first is obviously incomplete.

Alternatively, if you suspect that one particular document or class of documents has not been disclosed, seek an order for particular discovery requiring the opponent to swear an affidavit confirming whether he or she has the document(s) (RSC Ord 24, r 7). The application is on summons, with an affidavit stating your belief that the party has or had the document(s) described and that they are relevant to the case. On receipt of the affidavit you can then serve the maker with a notice to produce the document (see 8.2.1.)

If such orders are still not obeyed, the usual sanction is to apply to the court on summons for an order that the claim or defence shall be struck out unless the discovery is given within a stated time.

7.4   Discovery in the county court (CCR Ord 14)

There is no automatic discovery in the county court. Before applying to the court for an order, the party wanting discovery should ask the opponent in writing. If this is not complied with, then apply on notice to the court, usually at the pre-trial review (see 7.2). The list and affidavit are similar to those in the High Court. Use Oyez Forms N265 and N265(1).

Otherwise, the position is the same as in the High Court.

7.5   Non-party discovery

See Supreme Court Act 1981, s 34(2); RSC Ord 24, r 7A(2); County Courts Act 1984, s 53; CCR Ord 13, r 7; *O'Sullivan* v *Herdmans Ltd* [1987] 3 All ER 129, HL.

This procedure is available once a personal injury action (including an action for medical negligence) is under way to obtain discovery of particular relevant documents in the possession of people who are not parties to the action, for example medical records in the possession of a hospital in an ordinary road accident case.

The procedure is similar to that for particular discovery under RSC Ord 24, r 7 or CCR Ord 14, save that the summons states that the

application is made under RSC Ord 24, r 7A or CCR Ord 13, r 7 and
is served on the non-party as if it were a writ or county court summons
and on the other parties to the action. The party seeking discovery
will normally have to pay the non-party's costs.

7.6 Common problems and their solutions

Problem	Solution
Client suggests destruction/ concealment of relevant documents.	Warn that if client persists you cannot continue to act for him/her.
Suggestion in a medical report that plaintiff is malingering.	If in plaintiff's report, take client's instructions and ask doctor to amend report or put remarks in covering letter. Consider obtaining another report (if client or Legal Aid Board agree)— first report privileged. Otherwise, apply to court for leave to use report without prior disclosure. If in opponent's report obtain further medical evidence; seek evidence of previous illness eg sick notes for absence from work.
Defendant refuses to allow inspection of document claiming privilege.	If list inadequately states grounds for claiming privilege apply on summons or notice and affidavit for order for production of document for inspection. If grounds prima facie adequate serve notice requiring affidavit verifying list (Oyez Form B13) or apply for particular discovery. Court will inspect and rule on claim.
Hospital not involved in the case refuses to disclose documents.	Threaten or make application for non-party discovery; seek order for

	costs against hospital (*Hall v Wandsworth Health Authority* [1985] *Law Society's Gazette* 1329.
Opponent sends you privileged documents by mistake.	If mistake obvious you cannot use them (*Guinness Peat Properties* v *Fitzroy Robinson* [1987] 2 All ER 716, CA).

CHAPTER 8

PREPARING FOR TRIAL

This chapter considers the final steps needed to assemble the evidence, and arrange for the case to be listed for trial and tried. As the trial itself is likely to be handled either by counsel or by a solicitor with some experience it will not be dealt with here. (In any event, only a tiny proportion of cases go to a hearing: see Chapter 9). For more detail on evidence, see Cowsill and Clegg, *Evidence, Law and Practice*. On preparations generally, see O'Hare and Hill, *Civil Litigation* or Pritchard, *Personal Injury Litigation*.

8.1 Instructing counsel to advise on evidence

It is often useful to have counsel's advice on evidence at an early stage, or at least before the automatic directions, in case there is any need to seek different directions. However, in a case that will be argued by counsel it is highly desirable for counsel to assess the available evidence at the latest once discovery is complete and before the trial is in prospect. This is likely to be particularly important in more complex factory cases where there is, perhaps, a conflict of engineering evidence.

On how to instruct counsel, see 4.6. Counsel will particularly need to see the proofs of evidence, documents disclosed on discovery, reports from experts, the police or the Health and Safety Executive, plans and photographs and an updated schedule of special damages. The advice should identify the witnesses to be called and the documents to be used and deal with any other outstanding matters such as hearsay notices, notices to admit etc.

8.2 Documentary evidence

8.2.1 Notices to admit or produce documents (RSC Ord 27; CCR Ord 20) There may well be documents which the other party is unlikely to dispute if satisfied they are genuine, eg letters from the DHSS and other special damage documentation. In order to avoid having to call the writers to prove this, the notice to admit documents requires the opponent to admit the genuineness of the document referred to; if notice of non-admission is not given the opponent is deemed to admit their authenticity. In the High Court a notice to admit in Oyez Form B12AB should be served within twenty-one days of setting down the action for trial (see 8.6) and the notice of non-admission within a further twenty-one days. In the county court, notice to admit must be served at least fourteen days before the trial and notice of non-admission within seven days.

Note that it is not necessary to serve a notice to admit documents in the High Court if they have been disclosed on discovery, since the party given disclosure is deemed served with a notice to admit the documents disclosed (RSC Ord 27, r 4). It should, however, be considered in respect of documents coming to light or into existence later. In the county court the notice to admit documents procedure is not so likely to be needed as all documents appearing to be genuine are presumed genuine unless the other party takes objection (CCR Ord 20, r 11).

Remember also that it is normally necessary to use original and not copy documents. If the original is in the possession of a non-party, then that person can be served with a subpoena duces tecum or witness summons (see 8.3.2). If, however, the original is in the hands of your opponent, then you should serve a notice to produce the original at the trial (Oyez Form B10AB). The time limits are the same as for the notice to admit documents. However, the sanction is that if the opponent fails to produce the original you may use a copy or other secondary evidence (RSC Ord 27, r 5; CCR Ord 20, r 3 (4)).

8.2.2 Experts' reports Ensure that your expert evidence is no more than a year old at most and if necessary obtain an updating report. Ensure that the directions for using such evidence have been obtained where necessary (see Chapter 7) and complied with. Try and agree the reports if possible. It may be helpful for experts, particularly non-medical experts, to have a 'without prejudice' meeting before the trial in order to identify the areas in dispute and the High Court may now order this (RSC Ord 38, r 38).

8.2.3 Plans and photographs These should be exchanged and agreed if possible. For the position regarding plans more elaborate than mere sketch plans see 7.1.2.

8.2.4 Previous convictions etc Ask the defendant to admit the fact of the conviction if this has not already been done in the defence. If necessary, a notice to admit the fact can be served (see 8.3.1). As a precaution, obtain the certificate of conviction from the criminal court concerned. Ask the defendant to agree that the coroner's notes of any inquest should be admissible.

8.2.5 Agreeing bundles of documents In the more complex personal injury cases, particularly factory cases, there may be documentary evidence beyond the experts' reports, such as safety committee minutes. The plaintiff's solicitor should prepare bundles of documents that the parties agree are relevant to the case. At least seven sets will be needed where counsel is appearing on both sides since copies are needed for solicitors and counsel on both sides, for the judge, the witness giving evidence and the client. The bundles should be in chronological order, with the oldest at the top and the newest at the bottom. Ensure that the pagination is agreed with your opponent and carefully followed.

8.3 Witnesses

8.3.1 Avoiding the attendance of witnesses Always try to avoid having to call witnesses by attempting to agree the evidence with your opponent. A means of putting pressure on the opponent to do so is to serve a notice to admit facts in Oyez Form B53 (High Court) or N281 (county court). The time limits are as for the notice to admit documents (see 8.2.1). The sanction is that if the party served with the notice fails to admit the facts specified he or she will be liable for the opponent's costs in proving them unless the court otherwise orders (for example, because the facts in question were hotly disputed and were not such that the party served should reasonably have admitted) (RSC Ord 27, r 2; CCR Ord 20, r 2). Thus a notice could be served requiring the defendant to admit to having been involved in the accident. If the defendant failed to admit this, he or she would be liable to pay the cost of proving it even if it was held at the trial that the defendant was not negligent.

If a witness is seriously ill, has died or is going abroad for a long time, or cannot reasonably be expected to remember the events in question, then you should have grounds under the Civil Evidence Act 1968, s 8 for using a written statement or other hearsay evidence such as that of another person to whom the original witness spoke. Normally, such evidence must be 'first hand' hearsay, ie what A told B about events that A had personally perceived, if B's evidence is to be admissible under Civil Evidence Act 1968, s 2. However, more remote hearsay is admissible if it forms part of a record, ie it was compiled by a person acting under a duty from information supplied by a person with personal knowledge of the events (s 4).

If you wish to use such hearsay evidence, then you must follow the procedure laid down in RSC Ord 38, rr 7, 20–34 and CCR Ord 20, rr 14–26. Serve notice of your intention of doing so, in the *White Book* Editorial Form EF1 (hearsay statement), EF2 (oral hearsay statement) or EF3 (record) for both High Court and county court. The time limits are the same as for the notice to admit documents. The opponent can serve a counter-notice in form EF5 requiring the witness to attend. If you have alleged the existence of a s 8 ground then you should apply on summons or notice for the court to decide whether this is made out. If the court decides that it is, then the hearsay evidence can go in as of right. If the court decides there is no s 8 ground, or if none has been alleged, the service of a counter-notice will mean that the witness has to be called unless the court in its discretion orders otherwise.

8.3.2   Witnesses who need to attend   In respect of those witnesses who will need to attend the trial, including the client, it is important to send them in good time before the·case may be heard an updated proof of evidence for them to check and amend if necessary. As this will be the basis of the advocate's examination in chief of the witness, it should not contain any inadmissible material such as non-expert opinion or hearsay not covered by the Civil Evidence Act. Ask the witness to sign and date the proof in case he should die or become seriously ill before the trial, since the proof would then be admissible under the 1968 Act.

Also find out whether the witness is likely to attend the trial voluntarily. If there is some doubt about this, or in some cases, if it will help the witness (such as some expert witnesses) to break other commitments, serve the witness with a subpoena (High Court) or witness summons (county court) (RSC Ord 38, r 14; CCR Ord 20, r 12). These may require the witness to attend to give evidence (subpoena ad testificandum) or to produce a document (subpoena duces tecum).

To obtain a subpoena, lodge at court a completed form of praecipe (Oyez Form E20) and subpoena (Oyez Form G1/2). The subpoena must then be served personally on the witness within twelve weeks with conduct money covering travelling expenses and subsistence. To obtain a witness summons, lodge a form of request (Oyez Form N286) and the witnesses' expenses. The witness may be served either personally or by post, a reasonable time before the trial.

8.4 Real evidence

Ensure that arrangements are made to bring to court vital objects that the judge may want to see in order to understand what is alleged to have occurred, eg the defective brake part or the piece of machinery alleged to have caused the injury. If this is not feasible, eg because of their size, and the position cannot be adequately explained by photographs, then agree with the other side that it will be necessary for the judge to view the object and/or accident scene in person (RSC Ord 35, r 8; CCR Ord 21, r 6).

8.5 Other pre-setting down points

Because of the recent change in the High Court procedure for setting down cases for trial (see 8.6) it is now vital that the case should be ready to be heard as soon as it is set down. In the county court you will probably not be given a trial date until you have lodged a certificate of readiness, but if the defendant is dilatory then the plaintiff can apply for a hearing date; if the plaintiff is slow the defendant can apply for the action to be dismissed. The other matters that may need attention are listed below.

8.5.1 Compliance with directions for trial. Keep up the pressure on your opponent and apply for the action to be dismissed or defence to be struck out unless the orders are complied with within the time fixed in the automatic directions or ordered by the court.

8.5.2 Possible settlement of the claim It is still likely that the case will settle, even if only at the door of the court. However, beware the pressure that can be brought to bear on a plaintiff who has never been through court proceedings before.

8.5.3 Updating the special damages calculation Once updated figures are prepared the plaintiff should try to agree them with the defence. Service of a notice to admit documents or a notice of intention of using hearsay evidence may encourage agreement.

In the High Court the plaintiff must then prepare a schedule of special damages, including loss of earnings, loss of earning capacity, medical expenses and loss of pension rights. This must be served on the defendant in a Principal Registry case within seven days of the case appearing in the warned list or within twenty-eight days of any date fixed for the trial. In a district registry case it must be served on setting down the case for trial (*Practice Direction (Damages: Personal Injuries)* [1984] 1 WLR 1127 as modified by *Directions for Trial Out of London 31 July 1987* (1987) NLJ 733). The defendant then has fourteen days in which to state to what extent these are agreed and any counter-proposals.

8.5.4 Notice of intention to proceed after a year's delay By RSC Ord 3, r 6 one month's notice of intention to proceed must be given in the High Court if a year or more has elapsed since the last step was taken. A letter will suffice or Oyez Form B 85. In cases of serious delay by a plaintiff the defendant may then consider an application to dismiss the action for want of prosecution: see 9.4.

8.5.5 Removal of any limitations on any legal aid certificate Legal aid is quite often limited in personal injury cases to cover all steps up to but excluding setting down for trial. Obtain counsel's opinion that the case is suitable for trial and ask the Legal Aid Board to remove the limitation.

8.5.6 Briefing counsel Because of the need to be ready for trial as soon as the case is set down, it is advisable to prepare the brief in High Court cases at this stage. You will normally wish to use the counsel who has been advising throughout, but the brief should be a full one so that the case can be taken over if necessary by a counsel who has not previously been involved.

The brief should enclose the writ and pleadings, reports, agreed bundles of documents, a schedule of special damages and previous opinions of counsel. It should outline the facts and the issues in dispute, the evidence and any difficulties with it, and any particularly salient or recent developments in the relevant law. For a specimen brief see O'Hare and Hill, *Civil Litigation*, pp 402–406.

As the brief fee becomes due on delivery of the brief, it is wise to delay actual submission of the brief until after setting down. Additionally, the plaintiff may wish to take advantage of the forthcoming increase in the expense of the case by putting pressure on the defendant to settle. This can be done by the plaintiff writing to the defendant indicating that the brief will be delivered unless a satisfactory offer in settlement is made within a stated time.

If no settlement is forthcoming, it will then be necessary to deliver the brief and, in a non-legal aid case, to agree the brief fee. This is done over the telephone with counsel's clerk, professional ethics preventing counsel from dealing with the matter.

It may also be helpful for counsel to meet the client in conference at his chambers if this has not already occurred. This will convey to counsel the client's likely calibre as a witness, it should give the client added confidence in the person who will be his or her representative at the trial; and sometimes it can bring home to the client the difficulties in the case more effectively than advice from the solicitor with whom there is continuing contact.

8.6 Setting down the case for trial (RSC Ord 34)

The following procedure applies only to the High Court. In the county court a hearing date may have already been fixed at the pre-trial review. If it has not, then a date will be fixed on the parties lodging a certificate of readiness stating that the directions made at the pre-trial review have been complied with, and an estimate of the time their case is likely to take.

8.6.1 Setting down procedure See also *Directions for Trial Out of London 31 July 1987*, (1987) *Gazette Digest* July–September p 57.

Within the time stated in the automatic directions or order for directions send or take to court:

- Letter requesting action be set down.
- Two bundles in the following order:

    (a) any notice of issue of legal aid;
    (b) writ, pleadings and any further and better particulars;
    (c) any orders for directions;
    (d) any third party documents (from the defendant);
    (e) statement of parties (this certifies that directions have been complied with; whether experts' reports have been agreed and if not how many experts will be called; estimates the length of the trial (agreed if possible) and gives the names, addressés and telephone numbers of the parties, the solicitors and counsel. This forms the backsheet to the bundle. The title to the action should appear on the frontsheet.

- Cheque payable to HMPG for the fee (see 10.1.1).

Additionally, a copy of any agreed experts' reports must be lodged at court by the plaintiff within fourteen days of agreement or as soon after setting down as practicable.

If the plaintiff does not set the case down in the time ordered the defendant can do so or apply to have the action dismissed (see 9.4). The party setting down must give notice of having done so to the other parties in Oyez Form B14B within twenty-four hours of setting down.

8.6.2   Transfer to the county court (CCR Ord 16, r 6) If the case is set down under the automatic directions the court must consider whether to exercise its powers under County Courts Act 1984, s 40 to transfer cases suitable for determination by the county court regardless of the amount of the claim. Although the powers can be used whatever the views of the parties, they must have the chance of being heard on the point (RSC Ord 107, r 2). In order to clear the recent large backlog of Queen's Bench cases such transfer has become increasingly common. See also *Practice Direction (County Court: Transfer of Action from the Queen's Bench Division)* [1988] 2 All ER 64.

8.6.3   Listing arrangements These will not normally cause problems in the county court since a fixed date will always be given. The problem there is rather that if the fixed date proves too short a time for the case to be completed, then it will have to be adjourned until the next occasion when the judge is sitting in that place and a court is free.

In High Court district registry actions, on setting down the court will inform the parties approximately when the action will be heard, bearing in mind that in most court centres High Court judges will only be available for certain periods of the year. The client and witnesses should be asked to keep this period free of commitments if possible. You are likely to receive very short notice of the actual hearing date so you may well have to inform the client and witnesses personally or by telephone.

In the Principal Registry the case will on setting down normally go into the Non-Jury General List unless the time estimated for it does not exceed four hours, when it will go into the Short Cause List (*Practice Direction: Trials in London* [1981] 1 WLR 1296). The court issues Weekly Lists and also Daily Cause Lists with warned lists of cases expected to be taken the next day. These should be watched carefully so as to give the client and witnesses the maximum notice possible of the hearing. The average delay between setting down and hearing has now been reduced to three months (*Practice Direction (Listing)* (1988) *The Independent*, 29 March). This has been achieved by a rigorous approach to requests to take cases out of the list on the ground that one or both parties are not ready. The court may dismiss the action even if both parties are agreeable to the delay (*Rezael* v *Zelin and Zelin* (1988) NLJ 70). It is also vital to inform the court if the case settles or there is some real reason for delay, such as illness of a party or witness.

It may be convenient to avoid the uncertainties of knowing when the trial will take place in the High Court by applying for a fixed date. This will be particularly convenient if there are many expert witnesses, although the client should be warned that the price of certainty may be a rather longer wait than if he or she had simply waited his or her turn in the queue. In London, apply within twenty-eight days of setting down to the Clerk of the Lists for an appointment, and give notice on Oyez Form B14D to the other parties. Consider carefully, however, whether the application is really necessary (*Practice Direction (Listing)* (1988) *The Independent*, 29 March). Outside London apply to the district registrar within seven days of setting down either jointly or, if on the application of one party alone, then on seven days' notice to other parties.

8.6.4 Exchange lists of authorities If cases are to be cited, then exchange lists of authorities and notify the court in good time before the trial. This is particularly important in the county court and district registries which may not have easy access to law reports.

8.7 The trial (RSC Ord 35; CCR Ord 21)

8.7.1 The solicitor's role This book assumes that the reader will not personally be presenting cases in either the High Court or the county court. The reader's role will thus be the minor but nevertheless important one of ensuring the attendance at court of the client and witnesses. Once at court, it will be necessary to liaise between the client and witnesses, on the one hand, and counsel (who cannot discuss the case with the witnesses) on the other. It will also be necessary to take a note of the evidence, particularly when your advocate is on his or her feet.

8.7.2 After the judgment It is important to remind the advocate to ask the judge to deal with the following matters where appropriate:

- Interest on the damages.
- Costs against the opponent. Remember to ask the judge to deal with any interlocutory applications where costs were reserved, and to point out where your client is entitled to costs whatever the outcome eg because of service of a notice to admit).
- Order for legal aid taxation of your own costs, whatever the outcome of the case.
- Payment into court. This may substantially affect the entitlement to costs.
- Stay of execution for a stated period pending an appeal.

8.7.3 Remaining matters The following points may need attention:

- Drawing up the judgment (RSC Ord 42). In the High Court the successful party must prepare the judgment in Oyez Form D11, following the findings of the judge as recorded in the associate's certificate. The judgment and copy must be taken to the Action Department (Judgment Room) in Principal Registry cases or sent to the district registry with the associate's certificate, original writ, pleadings and list of exhibits. The court will then seal and return one copy of the judgment, which must then be served on the other side.

- Appeal (Supreme Court Act 1981, s 18; RSC Ord 59; County Courts Act 1984, ss 77–81). Notice of appeal will have to be given to the Court of Appeal within four weeks in Oyez Form B78. Leave of the Court of Appeal will not normally be needed where final judgment has been entered in a personal injury action. However, you will need to seek counsel's advice on the wisdom of an appeal and he will need to settle the grounds of appeal as these must be drafted with care. See O'Hare and Hill, *Civil Litigation*, Chapter 23.

- Taxation of costs. The judge will usually order that costs be taxed if not agreed. Try to agree costs, but if this is not possible remember to submit your bill for taxation within three months. See 3.1.1.

8.8 Common problems and their solutions

Problem	*Solution*
Defendant delays agreeing special damages documents.	Plaintiff threatens/serves notice to admit special damage or notice of intention of using such documents as hearsay evidence on grounds that authors cannot reasonably be expected to remember the information in them.
Witness reluctant to attend court.	Remind witness that damages will be paid by insurers. Take signed and dated proof of evidence. Threaten/serve subpoena or witness summons. Once in witness box can be cross-

	examined on proof if proves hostile.
Plaintiff late in setting action down for trial	Defendant sets action down or applies for it to be dismissed for want of prosecution (see 9.4).
Plaintiff's medical condition still not stable at setting down stage.	Consider applying for split trial, liability only being dealt with at this stage. But disadvantageous to plaintiff if case strong on quantum but weak on liability.
Court refuses fixed date for trial.	Ask court to list case as not to be heard before a particular date (to suit parties or witnesses) or (in London) accept offer to supply fixed date on short notice while staying in Non-Jury General List.
Judgment entered or case dismissed because one party failed to appear at trial (RSC Ord 35, r 1; CCR Ord 21, rr 1, 3).	Apply on summons/ notice within seven days for the judgment to be set aside (usually granted on condition that applicant pays costs of the abortive trial) (RSC Ord 35, r 2; CCR Ord 37, r 2).

CHAPTER 9

EARLY CONCLUSION OF CASES

This chapter will consider the commonest ways in which personal injury actions may terminate without the need for a trial, as indeed is the case in the great majority of actions.

For more detail see O'Hare and Hill, *Civil Litigation* or Pritchard, *Personal Injury Litigation*.

9.1 Settlement before or after proceedings issued

9.1.1 Settlement before proceedings have commenced Most personal injury cases are settled without the need to start proceedings. The settlement terms are recorded in the correspondence between the solicitors and insurers. The latter may ask the plaintiff to sign a receipt confirming acceptance of the payment in full and final settlement of the claim. As problems of enforcement of settlements rarely arise in personal injury actions no other formalities are needed except in the case of minors and other people under a disability such as mental patients, where the court will have to approve the settlement (see 9.2).

However, it is important to explain the effect of a proposed settlement to the client, particularly the impact where relevant of the Legal Aid Board charge. It will be wise to obtain counsel's opinion on the proposed settlement in substantial cases. Obtain written confirmation from the client that he or she understands and accepts the settlement terms. Finally, ensure that the position as to costs has been agreed.

9.1.2 Settlement after proceedings have commenced
- Informing the court. If the case has been set down for trial in the High Court the court must be informed of the settlement and the parties should jointly apply to withdraw the action from the list. If the case has not been set down the court need not be informed.
- Is a court order desirable? An order has the advantages of certainty, and it will allow for costs to be taxed if they have not been agreed. The usual procedure is to obtain a stay of the proceedings, freezing them either temporarily or, once all the terms

of the settlement have been agreed, permanently, except for the possibility of returning to court to ensure the carrying out of any of the terms agreed (a 'Tomlin' order). The order should also refer to any interim payments already made, provide for payment out of any money in court, deal with which party is to receive the interest on money in court, and for costs between the parties and for taxation of any legally aided party's costs.

• Obtaining the consent order. In High Court cases, the plaintiff prepares the draft order, asks the defendant to indorse his consent and sends it to the court, which seals it and returns it to the plaintiff. The plaintiff sends a copy to the defendant who should then forward any outstanding monies to the plaintiff.

In the county court, the plaintiff will prepare a notice of application for judgment to be entered in the agreed terms, obtain the defendant's consent and then lodge it at court. The court will send sealed copies to both parties.

• Money in court. To take the money out of the High Court the plaintiff sends to the court the consent order, the stamped notice of payment in, two copies of the payment schedule (Oyez Form B84) and a form of request for payment out of court (Oyez Form B80).

The county court will send the money in court to the plaintiff's solicitor on the making of the consent order.

9.2 Persons under a disability

When settling claims on behalf of minors and mental patients, the court's approval to the settlem̄ t will be needed before the settlement can be accepted if proceedings have started (RSC Ord 80, r 10; CCR Ord 10, r 10). This is also so in fatal cases where a payment into court has to be apportioned between the 1934 and 1976 Act claims and/or between dependants. It is also desirable to obtain such approval even if no proceedings have been needed in order to protect the next friend from any later suggestion that the plaintiff has been under-compensated. It is not wise to accept any suggestion by insurers that payment should be made simply against a receipt signed by the next friend; indeed, the insurers should be prepared to pay the plaintiff's costs in obtaining the court's approval.

The plaintiff should issue and serve a minor settlement summons in Oyez Form S20 following the usual procedure (see Chapter 7.1). If no proceedings have been started, a minor settlement originating summons will be needed in Oyez Form S20B. For the court fee see Chapter 10. The procedure is the same as for issuing a writ. On issue the court supplies a form of request for directions as to investment. The originating summons must be served at least four days before the hearing. The defendant does not need to acknowledge service. In the county court the application for the court's approval is made by a notice of application following the usual procedure.

In each case, the parties will attend the hearing. The plaintiff will outline the allegations and the evidence available to prove them, and produce to the court the experts' reports and, in cases of difficulty, counsel's opinion on the acceptability of the proposed settlement. The master will then be told the proposed settlement figure and will decide if it is reasonable given the risks of litigation.

If the master does not approve the settlement, then he or she can give further directions for the conduct of the rest of the case. However, if it is approved, then the master will give directions as to investment until the plaintiff reaches eighteen. The next friend can, however, apply for payment of expenses and for payments for the child's benefit, such as alterations to the home or a holiday to help recuperation. If the plaintiff is a mental patient the settlement monies will usually be transferred to the Court of Protection.

The Court must approve costs payable by the defendant to the plaintiff or tax them if not agreed. The plaintiff's solicitor in a non-legally aided case will usually waive any claim for further costs.

9.3 Default judgments; summary judgment

9.3.1 Default judgments (RSC Ords 13, 19; CCR Ord 9) Judgment can be obtained in both the High Court and county court if the defendant fails to serve or file a Defence (RSC Ord 19; CCR Ord 9) within the proper time. In the High Court judgment can also be obtained if the defendant fails to return the acknowledgment of service in time or immediately if the defendant returns it indicating that the action will not be defended. (RSC Ord 13). Such judgment will be interlocutory judgment on liability with damages and interest to be assessed later and costs to be taxed.

In the High Court the procedure is to send or take to the court office the following:

• The original writ.
• An affidavit of service or acknowledgment of service (if the defendant has failed to give notice of intention to defend) or original statement of claim (if the defendant has failed to file a defence).
• Three copies of judgment form (Oyez Form D2).

The sealed judgment will be handed or sent to the plaintiff.

In the county court, if the defendant has not filed a Defence on time the plaintiff may obtain judgment simply by lodging Oyez Form N234 (unless the claim is only for the cost of road accident repairs since this is treated as a liquidated claim and Oyez Form N14 is used).

Note that the leave of the court will be needed if the defendant is under a disability or the plaintiff is claiming provisional damages.

Such default judgments may be set aside on the application of the defendant on summons or notice and affidavit in support. This will be as of right if there has been an irregularity such as improper service of the writ or summons, but otherwise in the discretion of the court. The defendant will usually have to show a good reason for allowing the judgment to be entered (such as illness) and that there is a possible defence.

9.3.2 Summary judgment (RSC Ord 14; CCR Ord 9, r 14) Summary judgment will not very often be available in a personal injuries case since there will often be some argument on contributory negligence. However, in a case where it seems clear to the plaintiff that there can be no real defence, or at least a defence only on the extent of the damages, it may be worth applying for summary judgment. Even if the defendant obtains leave to defend it will put pressure on the defendant. The court will also give directions for the rest of the case. If the plaintiff obtains judgment, it will be on liability only, with damages and interest to be assessed and costs to be taxed. See RSC Ord 14.

In the High Court, the plaintiff can apply as soon as the statement of claim has been served and the defendant has given notice of intention to defend. Apply on summons (use Oyez Form S3) with an affidavit in Oyez Form B34/34A. These must be served on the defendant at least ten clear days before the hearing. The defendant can serve an affidavit in reply at least three days before the hearing.

In the county court, the application should be made once the defendant has filed a document purporting to be a defence. The application is by notice of application served with a copy of the affidavit in Oyez Form CC1014 on the defendant at least seven days before the hearing. The application will usually be heard at the pre-trial review. See CCR Ord 9, r 14.

9.3.3 Judgment on admissions If the defendant clearly admits both liability and the fact that the plaintiff has suffered some damage, whether in the pleadings, correspondence or otherwise, the plaintiff can apply on summons or notice for such judgment, to which he or she may be entitled, to be entered. This will normally be judgment on liability only as above. See RSC Ord 27, r 3; CCR Ord 7, r 6.

9.3.4   Assessment of damages   In the High Court follow RSC Ord 37:

1 Send to district registry or Action Department, Royal Courts of Justice or take to district registry or Room 122, Royal Courts of Justice: sealed copy of the judgment. Cheque payable to HMPG for the fee (see Chapter 10.1.1).
  Special Appointment Form (Pritchard, *Personal Injury Litigation*, Precedent 6).
2 Court sends/gives notice of appointment to plaintiff.
3 Plaintiff serves notice of appointment on defendant at least seven days before hearing.
4 Master makes order and indorses on the copy judgment.
5 Plaintiff attends Room 122, Royal Courts of Justice or district registry with copy judgment and amount of damages inserted.

In the county court follow CCR Ord 22, r 6:

1 Plaintiff takes or sends to the court notice of application for assessment of damages.
2 Court indorses details of hearing and returns notice to plaintiff.
3 Plaintiff serves notice on defendant at least seven days before hearing.
4 Parties attend hearing before the judge.
5 Court draws up judgment and sends it to the parties.

9.4   Striking out, dismissal for want of prosecution, discontinuance

9.4.1 Striking out pleadings and general writ indorsements   By RSC Ord 18, r 19; CCR Ord 13, r 5 this can be done if:

• The pleading or indorsement discloses no reasonable cause of action or defence (no evidence can be adduced to show this), or
• The pleading or indorsement is scandalous, frivolous or vexatious (a far too prolix pleading might be vexatious), or
• The pleading or indorsement may prejudice, embarrass or delay the fair trial of the action, eg because the pleading is unclear, or
• The pleading or indorsement is otherwise an abuse of process of the court.
  Apply on summons or notice as soon as the offending pleading has

been served giving the grounds and stating exactly what you want the court to do. The court will only strike out a pleading and dismiss the action or enter judgment in a clear case. In other cases it will usually allow the party concerned to amend the pleading. However, even if the action continues it can be a means of putting pressure on your opponent.

9.4.2 Dismissal for want of prosecution The courts have power to do this inherently and under several rules. This is a key defence tactic to deal with cases which the plaintiff accidentally or deliberately has let 'go to sleep', although it is not used as much as formerly. The defendant can apply for the action to be dismissed for want of prosecution if it can be shown that the plaintiff's delay is either intentional and contumelious (insolent), eg deliberate disobedience to a peremptory order of the court; or that it is inordinate, inexcusable and prejudicial to the fair trial of the action. The whole period of the delay must be looked at and the nearer the limitation period is to expiry the quicker the plaintiff must act. However, if the limitation period has not expired, the action will not usually be dismissed since the plaintiff could start another action (*Birkett* v *James* [1978] AC 297).

9.4.3 Discontinuance and withdrawal (RSC Ord 21; CCR Ord 18) In both the High Court and the county court the defendant can withdraw the defence at any time without the leave of the court (RSC Ord 21; CCR Ord 18). The plaintiff can tax his costs.

The plaintiff's position varies between the High Court and the county court. In the High Court, the plaintiff can discontinue by giving notice of discontinuance in Oyez Form B19. If this is done within fourteen days of service of the defence, the leave of the court is not needed. The defendant will be entitled to costs. If the plaintiff wishes to discontinue after this point, or after an interim payment has been made, or if the plaintiff wishes to avoid paying the defendant's costs, then the court's leave must be sought.

In the county court the plaintiff can discontinue by serving notice in Oyez Form N279 at any time before judgment. Leave to discontinue is never needed. However, the defendant will be entitled to tax his costs unless the court orders otherwise.

Accordingly, it is wise for the client to think carefully before starting or defending an action without a clear indication that success is likely.

9.5   Common problems and their solutions

Problem	*Solution*
Term of settlement not complied with.	Party returns to court under liberty to apply reserved in judgment. Otherwise start fresh action to enforce contract of compromise.
Plaintiff enters judgment in default.	Defendant applies for judgment to be set aside if able to show good reason for allowing judgment to be entered and possible defence.
Plaintiff serves summary judgment application.	Defendant serves affidavit in reply and (High Court) prepares draft Defence if possible (already served in county court). Defendant should consider making a payment into court.
Major defects in a pleading.	Suggest other party amends pleading. In default apply for pleading to be struck out. If court allows amendment, seek costs.
Lengthy delays in plaintiff's case.	Defendant should consider applying for dismissal for want of prosecution, at least as soon as limitation period expired. Before this, defendant can seek peremptory order that action be dismissed unless required step taken within stated time (any later proceedings will be stayed as abuse of process). Plaintiff can reduce chance of successful application to dismiss by proceeding as fast as possible and informing defendant of reason for any delay.

CHAPTER 10

FEES AND USEFUL ADDRESSES

10.1 High Court fees, room numbers and telephone numbers

10.1.1 Court fees

Issuing writ	£60
Originating summons—minor approval	£10
Originating summons—other	£60
Setting down for trial	£30
Assessment of damages (after judgment)	£15
Appeal to judge in chambers	£15
Non-consent summons	£10
Taxation of costs—amount allowed—not over £500	£25
—over £500	5p per £1

10.1.2 RCJ room numbers The address of the Royal Courts of Justice is The Strand, London WC2A 2LL. The following rooms deal with most steps in QBD personal injury claims.

Action Department
- Writs and Acknowledgments of Service (01–936 6528 if A–H; 01–936 6614 if I–Z);

   Room 121 (A–H) and Room 127 (I–Z), for issue of Writs, Originating Summons, and Third Party Notices.

   Room 123 (A–H) and Room 125 (I–Z). Entry of, and search for Acknowledgment of Service.
- Judgments and executions (01–936 6351 for A–H; 01–936 6245 for I–Z)

   Room 119 (A–H) and Room 129 (I–Z). For entry of judgment and issue of writs of execution.
- Summonses and Orders (01–936 6918)

   Room 126 (A–Z) for the issue of all QBD summonses. Also for filing of affidavits of service of a writ, when entering judgment in default of Notice of Intention to Defend. For other affidavit's, see below.

   Room 130. For the drawing up and filing of master's (and judge's) orders made in chambers.

- Judge in chambers listing (01–936 6511)
  Room 128 (A–Z). All appointments with a judge in chambers.

Affidavits
- Room 81 (01–936 6018) for the filing of all affidavits sworn in the QBD. The only exception is for affidavits when entering a judgment in default of Notice of Intention to Defend, see above.

Masters' Secretary's Department (01–936 6474)
- Room 122. Deals with all secretarial works of QBD masters, including references to masters for trial; ex parte applications; infant approval summonses, etc.

Clerk of the Lists (01–936 6532)
- Rooms 419–420 for Clerk of the Lists general office, including appointments and enquiries.

10.2   County court fees

Plaint fee on issuing proceedings or originating application (including postal service of summons and interlocutory applications unless fee specifically prescribed):

Claim not exceeding £300	10p per £ claimed, minimum £7
Claim exceeding £300 but not exceeding £500	£37
Claim exceeding £500 or not limited in amount	£43
Bailiff service	£5
Appeal to judge from registrar	£10
Taxation of costs	£5p per £1 or part allowed

10.3   Counsel's fees for personal injuries cases

	Running down £	Other cases £
Statement of claim	31	42
Defence without counterclaim	25	37
Defence (simple admission)	11	11
Further and better particulars		
–request	18	18
–answer	22	22

Reply	22	24
Interrogatories and answers	36	36
Advice on evidence	50	50
Opinion (including opinion on appeal)	36	36
Opinion on liability	44	44
Opinion on quantum	42	42
Opinion on liability and quantum	66	66
Opinion on liability, quantum and evidence	110	110
Notice of appeal to Court of Appeal and counter-notice	42	42
Brief on summons before master	36	36

Conference fees
Junior counsel — first ½ hour £25
each subsequent ½ hour £15
Queen's counsel — first ½ hour £45
each subsequent ½ hour £22

10.4 Fees for police accident reports

	£
Full report	29.10
Sketch plan (if supplied separately)	12.90
One statement (if supplied separately)	12.90
Two or more statements (if supplied separately)	17.20
Photographs, per print	1.20
Interview with police officer	30.20

10.5 Useful addresses

Association of Consulting Engineers
Alliance House
12 Caxton Street
London SW1
Tel: 01–222 6557

Action for Victims of Medical Accidents
24 Southwark Street
London
SE1 1TY
Tel: 01–403 4744

Criminal Injuries Compensation Board
Whittington House
19–30 Alfred Place
Chenies Street
London
WC1E 7LG
Tel: 01–636 9501

Employment Medical Advisory Service
(Health and Safety Commission)
Baynards House
1–13 Chepstow Place
Westbourne Grove
London
W2 4TS
Tel: 01–229 3456

Medical Defence Union
3 Devonshire Place
London
W1N 2EA
Tel: 01–486 6181

Medical Protection Society
50 Hallam Street
London
W1N 6DE
Tel: 01–637 0541

Motor Insurers' Bureau
New Garden House
78 Hatton Garden
London
EC1N 8JQ
Tel: 01–242 0033

CHAPTER 11

BASIC PRECEDENTS

The following documents illustrate a straightforward High Court personal injury action where the plaintiff is likely to receive considerable damages since the defendant's driver has been convicted of careless driving as a result of his part in the accident. Vicarious liability is not in issue but contributory negligence is raised. This does not prevent the plaintiff seeking an order for an interim award of damages. It should be assumed that the action is settled without the need for a trial.

11.1 Document 1: general indorsement of claim (on back of writ)

'The Plaintiff claims damages for personal injuries, loss and damage caused by the negligent driving of the Defendants, their servant or agent at the junction of High Street and Market Street, Barchester on 1 December 1987, together with interest on damages under s 35A of the Supreme Court Act 1981 for such periods and at such rates as the Court thinks just.'

11.2 Document 2: statement of claim

IN THE HIGH COURT OF JUSTICE   1988–W–1021
QUEEN'S BENCH DIVISION
BARCHESTER DISTRICT REGISTRY
(Writ issued 3 March 1988)

BETWEEN

<table>
<tr><td style="text-align:center">ROBERT WHITE</td><td style="text-align:right">Plaintiff</td></tr>
<tr><td style="text-align:center">and</td><td></td></tr>
<tr><td style="text-align:center">SAUNDERS, KNOTT & CO. LTD</td><td style="text-align:right">Defendants</td></tr>
</table>

STATEMENT OF CLAIM

1 On 1 December 1987 at about 8.00 am the Plaintiff was driving his motorcycle along High Street Barchester in a northerly direction and had stopped at the junction with Market Street.

2 The Plaintiff was intending to turn right into Market Street and was stationary with his right hand indicator flashing.

3 A car owned by the Defendants and driven by the Defendants' servant or agent Brian Morris in the course of his employment was proceeding along Market Street in an easterly direction.

4 The Defendants' car turned right into High Street and collided with the Plaintiff's motorcycle.

5 The collision was caused by the negligence of the Defendants, their servant or agent.

PARTICULARS

Brian Morris was negligent in that he:
    failed to indicate that he intended to turn right;
    cut the corner;
    failed properly to steer the Defendant's vehicle so as to avoid colliding with the Plaintiff's vehicle.

6 The Plaintiff will rely on the fact that on the 12 April 1988 Brian Morris was convicted at Barchester Magistrates' Court of driving without due care and attention at Barchester on the 1 December 1987.

7 By reason of the Defendants' negligence the Plaintiff has suffered pain and injury, loss and damage. The Plaintiff's date of birth is 26 February 1966.

PARTICULARS OF INJURY

Colles fracture of left wrist
Compound fracture of left femur
The Plaintiff has been unable to resume work or his hobby of playing cricket.

PARTICULARS OF SPECIAL DAMAGE

Loss of earnings from 1 December 1987
to 1 April 1988 at the net rate of £600 per month (and continuing)

	£2400.00
Less statutory sick pay received	
17 weeks at £40.25 per week	£684.25
	£1715.75
Written off value of motorcycle	£750.00
Value of clothing etc damaged	
beyond repair	£100.00

Travelling expenses to and from hospital at £3.00 per visit (and continuing)	£108.00
Prescriptions	£42.00
	£2715.75

8 The Plaintiff is entitled to interest on damages under s 35A of the Supreme Court Act 1981 for such periods and at such rates as the Court thinks just.

AND the Plaintiff claims:

(1) damages

(2) interest under s 35A of the Supreme Court Act 1981 for such periods and at such rates as the Court thinks just.

JOHN DOE

SERVED on 4 April 1988 by Sharp and Keen of 1 Ship Street Barchester, Plaintiff's solicitors.

11.3   Document 3: defence and counterclaim

IN THE HIGH COURT OF JUSTICE   1988–W–1021
QUEEN'S BENCH DIVISION
BARCHESTER DISTRICT REGISTRY

BETWEEN

ROBERT WHITE   Plaintiff

and

SAUNDERS, KNOTT & CO. LTD   Defendants

DEFENCE

1 The Defendants admit that their car, driven by Brian Morris, their servant or agent in the course of his employment, collided with the Plaintiff's motorcycle at the junction of High Street and Market Street Barchester at about 8.00 am on 1 December 1987.

2 The Defendants further admit that Brian Morris was convicted of careless driving as alleged in paragraph 6 of the Statement of Claim.

3 The Defendants state that the collision was caused or contributed to by the negligence of the Plaintiff.

PARTICULARS

The Plaintiff failed to indicate his intention of turning right into Market Street.

The Plaintiff continued to turn into Market Street when he saw or should have seen the Defendants' car about to turn into his path.

4 No admission is made as to the alleged or any pain or injury, loss or damage or as to any entitlement to interest.

5 Save as previously expressly admitted, each and every allegation in the Statement of Claim is denied as if each were here set out at length and denied specifically.

COUNTERCLAIM

6 The Defendants repeat paragraphs 1 to 5 above.

7 By reason of the Plaintiff's negligence the Defendants have incurred, inconvenience, loss and damage.

PARTICULARS OF SPECIAL DAMAGE

Repairs to car	£50
Cost of hiring replacement car while repairs carried out	£150
	£650

8   The Defendants are entitled to interest on damages under s 35A of the Supreme Court Act 1981 for such periods and at such rates as the Court thinks just.

AND the Defendants claim:
> damages
> interest under s 35A of the Supreme Court Act 1981 for such periods and at such rates as the Court thinks just.

RACHEL ROE

SERVED on 4 May 1988 by Gradgrind & Co of Dorrit Chambers, Eldon Street, Barchester, Defendants' solicitors

11.4   Document 4: affidavit in support of interim payment application

IN THE HIGH COURT OF JUSTICE   1988–W–1021
QUEEN'S BENCH DIVISION
BARCHESTER DISTRICT REGISTRY

BETWEEN

ROBERT WHITE	Plaintiff
and	
SAUNDERS, KNOTT & CO. LTD	Defendants

I, ROBERT WHITE of 1 The Park, Barchester, maintenance fitter MAKE OATH and say as follows:

1 I am advised by my solicitors and believe that if this action proceeds to trial I will obtain judgment for substantial damages against the Defendants.

2 I refer to the pleadings in this action. As stated in the Statement of Claim, when the accident occurred I was driving my motor cycle when it was involved in a collision with a car belonging to the Defendants and driven by the Defendants' servant or agent. The Defendants admit that the collision occurred but deny liability.

3 As a result of the accident I have sustained extensive personal injuries, in particular serious injury to my left arm and shoulder. It is probable that I will suffer permanent disability. There is now produced to me and marked "RW.1" a medical report by Mr Dean Swift dated 1 February 1988 confirming the extent of my injuries.

4 I have suffered the following special damages as at the date of this affidavit:

Loss of earnings from 1 December 1987 to 1 May 1988 at the net rate of	
£600 per month (and continuing)	£3,600.00
Less statutory sick pay received 22 weeks at £40.25 per week	885.50
	£2,714.50
Written off value of motor cycle	750.00
Value of clothing etc damaged beyond repair	100.00
Travelling expenses to and from hospital at £3.00 per visit (and continuing)	132.00
Prescriptions	50.00
	£3,746.50

5 There is now produced to me the bundle of documents marked "RW.2" containing evidence confirming the calculation of special damages.

Sworn at 10 High Street Barchester this 18 day of May 1988

R. White

Before me G. Travels
A Solicitor
This Affidavit is filed on behalf of the Plaintiff.

CHAPTER 12

FURTHER READING

Substantive law

Charlesworth and Percy, *Negligence*, 7th edn (Sweet and Maxwell) 1983 and 1987 supplement

Bingham, *Motor Claims Cases*, 9th edn (Butterworths) 1986

Walker, *The Consumer Protection Act 1987* (Longman) 1987

Williams, *Criminal Injuries Compensation*, 2nd edn (Waterlows) 1986

Holyoak and Allen, *Civil Liability for Defective Premises* (Butterworths) 1982

Munkman, *Employers' Liability*, 10th edn (Butterworths) 1985

Jackson and Powell, *Professional Negligence*, 2nd edn (Sweet and Maxwell) 1987

Kemp, *Damages for Personal Injury and Death*, 3rd edn (Longman) 1986

Kemp and Kemp, *The Quantum of Damages* (Sweet and Maxwell) looseleaf

Pollard, *Social Welfare Law* (Longman) looseleaf

Procedure: general

O'Hare and Hill, *Civil Litigation*, 4th edn (Longman) 1986

Pritchard, *Personal Injury Litigation*, 5th edn (Longman) 1986

Goldrein and De Haas, *Personal Injury Practice and Precedents* (Butterworths) 1985

Humphreys' District Registry Practice, 24th edn (Longman) 1987

Blackford and Price, *County Court Practice Handbook*, 8th edn (Longman) 1987

Specific aspects

Josling, *Periods of Limitation*, 6th edn (Longman) 1986

Rigby, *Contentious Costs* (Longman) 1988

Radevsky, *Service of Documents* (Longman) 1982

Bullen Leake and Jacob, *Precedents of Pleadings in the Queen's Bench Division*, 12th edn (Sweet and Maxwell) 1975

Chitty. and Jacob, *Queen's Bench Forms*, 21st edn (Sweet and Maxwell) 1986

Butterworth's County Court Precedents and Pleadings, looseleaf

Evidence

Style and Hollander, *Documentary Evidence*, 2nd edn (Longman) 1987

Cowsill and Clegg, *Evidence, Law and Practice*, 2nd edn (Longman) 1987